Emotions Ninja for Teens
Mastering Feelings and Emotions with Ninja Life Hacks

This book is dedicated to my sons - Mikey, Kobe, and Jojo.

Also by Mary Nhin:

Resilient Ninja | Business Ninja | Emotions Ninja for Teens | Growth Mindset Ninja for Teens | Leadership Ninja for Teens | Self-Management Ninja for Teens | Self-Awareness Ninja for Teens | Social Awareness Ninja for Teens | Decision-MakingNinja for Teens | Relationship Ninja for Teens | Money Ninja for Teens | Angry Ninja | Inventor Ninja | Positive Ninja | Lazy Ninja | Helpful Ninja | Grumpy Ninja | Earth Ninja | Kind Ninja | Perfect Ninja | Anxious Ninja | Money Ninja | Gritty Ninja | Dishonest Ninja | Shy Ninja | Unplugged Ninja | Diversity Ninja | Inclusive Ninja | Masked Ninja | Grateful Ninja | Hangry Ninja | Focused Ninja | Calm Ninja | Brave Ninja | Worry Ninja | Funny Ninja | Patient Ninja | Organized Ninja | Communication Ninja | Stressed Ninja | Smart Ninja | Hopeful Ninja | Confident Ninja | Zen Ninja | Goal-setting | Lonely Ninja | Self-Disciplined Ninja | Motivated Ninja | Sad Ninja | Impulsive Ninja | Feelings Ninja | Creative Ninja | Forgetful Ninja | Nervous Ninja | Emotionally Intelligent Ninja | Growth Mindset Ninja | Jealous Ninja | Frustrated Ninja | Memory Ninja | Listening Ninja | Innovative Ninja | Supportive Ninja | Love Ninja | Humble Ninja | Quiet Ninja | Compassionate Ninja | Sharing Ninja | Caring Ninja | Curious Ninja | Hard-working Ninja | Investments | Problem-Solving Ninja | Integrity Ninja | Disappointed Ninja | eNinja | Healthy Ninja | Adaptable Ninja | Respectful Ninja | Flexible Thinking Ninja | Entrepreneur Ninja | Accountable Ninja | Consent Ninja | Negative Ninja | Sensory Ninja | Tired Ninja | Social Ninja | Neurodivergent Ninja | Happy Ninja | Visionary Ninja | Passionate Ninja | Honest Ninja | Authentic Ninja | Loyal Ninja | Debate Ninja | Collaborative Ninja | Distracted Ninja | Embarrassed Ninja | Negotiator Ninja | Cooperative Ninja | Furious Ninja | Scared Ninja | I Love You, Little Ninja | Gritty Ninja and the St. Patrick's Day Race | Kind Ninja and the Easter Egg Hunt | I Love You, Mom - Earth Ninja | I Love You, Dad - Grumpy Ninja | Patient Ninja's Halloween | Grateful Ninja's Thanksgiving | Ninja Life Hacks Christmas | Ninjas Know the CBT Triangle | Ninjas Go to the Dentist | Ninjas Go to Europe | Ninja Go Camping | Ninjas Go to the Library | Ninjas Go Through a Ninja Warrior Obstacle Course | Ninjas Go to a Party | Ninjas Go to Space | Ninjas Go to Work | Ninjas Go to School | Ninja Life Hacks Numbers | Ninja Life Hacks ABCs of Feelings | Ninja Life Hacks Shapes | Ninja Life Hacks Colors | Ninja Life Hacks Body Parts | Ninja Life Hacks Animals | Ninja Life Hacks Opposites | Ninja Life Hacks Weather | Unplugged Ninja in Vietnam |Kind Ninja Builds a Buddy Bench | Magical Mistake Machine | Lunar New Year | Happy Birthday Ninja | Ninja's New Year | Chef Ninja | Engineer Ninja | Teacher Ninja | Doctor Ninja | Firefighter Ninja | Police Officer Ninja | President Ninja | Coding Ninja | Neurologist Ninja | Amelia Earhart | Steve Jobs | Elon Musk | Indra Nooyi | Anne Frank | Serena Williams | Albert Einstein | Mae Jemison | Frida Kahlo | Michael Jordan | Jane Goodall | Helen Keller | Muhammad Ali | The Wright Brothers | Kobe Bryant | Rosa Parks | Ray Kroc | Martin Luther King, Jr. | Michelle Obama | Sara Blakely | Barack Obama | Walt Disney | Peggy Cherng | David Bowie | Mia Hamm | Sam Walton | Tiger Woods | Jackie Robinson | Mother Teresa | Harriet Tubman | Chloe Kim | Neil Armstrong | Ella Fitzgerald | Stevie Wonder | Maya Angelou | Wilma Rudolph | Lionel Messi | Cristiano Ronaldo | Sophie Cruz | Taylor Swift | Sonia Gandhi | Never Ever Marry a Mermaid | Never Ever Lick a Llama | Never Ever Upset a Unicorn | Never Ever Massage a Moose | Never Ever Dance with Dracula | Never Ever Tickle a Turkey | Never Ever Race a Reindeer

Emotions Ninja for Teens
Mastering Feelings and Emotions with Ninja Life Hacks

by Mary Nhin

Emotions Ninja for Teens: Mastering Feelings and Emotions with Ninja Life Hacks
© 2025 Mary Nhin | Ninja Life Hacks
All rights reserved.

No part of this book may be reproduced, distributed, or transmitted in any form or by any means, including photocopying, recording, or other electronic or mechanical methods, without the prior written permission of the publisher, except in the case of brief quotations embodied in critical reviews and certain other noncommercial uses permitted by copyright law.

For permission requests, please contact the publisher at:
Grow Grit Press LLC
info@ninjalifehacks.tv

First Edition: 2025
Paperback ISBN: 979-8-89614-070-2
Hardcover ISBN: 979-8-89614-072-6
eBook ISBN: 979-8-89614-071-9

Published by:
Grow Grit Press LLC

ninjalifehacks.tv

Disclaimer: The information provided in this book is based on the author's personal experiences and research. It is intended for educational and informational purposes only. The author and publisher make no guarantees of success or improvement from applying the strategies outlined in this book. Readers are encouraged to consult professionals before making health, financial, legal, or business decisions. Some stories in this book are inspired by real events or composite experiences from friends, students, etc. They're meant to illustrate typical teen challenges.

Printed in the United States of America.

TABLE OF CONTENTS

Foreword – By Dr. Emily Carter, Child Psychologist & Emotional Intelligence Educator	9
Author's Note – A Personal Message from the Author	12
Introduction – Understanding and Managing Your Emotions	14
Chapter 1: The Power of Kindness	17
Chapter 2: Managing Anger Before It Manages You	29
Chapter 3: Understanding the Connection Between Thoughts, Feelings, and Behaviors	41
Chapter 4: Managing Anxiety and Taking Control	53
Chapter 5: Unlocking the Science of Happiness	65
Chapter 6: Understanding and Processing Sadness	79
Chapter 7: The Power of Patience	89
Chapter 8: Overcoming Worry and Finding Peace	101
Chapter 9: Shifting Your Mindset	113
Chapter 10: Finding Calm in Chaos	123
Chapter 11: Building Self-Belief	135
Chapter 12: F.U.N. Steps to Speak Up	147
Final Thoughts – Your Journey to Emotional Strength	158
Final Reflections – Your Emotional Growth Journey	160
Ninja Moves Glossary	162
Help and Support Resources	166
Books & Resources Mentioned in This Book	172
About the Author	176

FOREWORD

Emotions are powerful. They can lift us up, push us forward, or sometimes feel like they are holding us back. As a child psychologist, I've seen firsthand how emotions shape the way young people experience the world. But here's something important, emotions are not the enemy. They are guides, signals, and tools for growth.

That's what makes *Emotions Ninja for Teens: Mastering Emotions with Ninja Life Hacks* such an essential book. It doesn't just explain emotions, it teaches practical, real-life strategies to navigate them in a healthy way. From managing anger to finding confidence, overcoming worry, and embracing kindness, this book is filled with actionable techniques that will help teens handle life's ups and downs with resilience and strength.

One of my favorite things about this book is its approachable and engaging format. Instead of overwhelming readers with theories, it provides relatable stories, personal experiences, and step-by-step methods known as Mary's ninja life hacks to help teens gain control over their emotional well-being. The strategies in these pages aren't just for now, they are skills that will last a lifetime.

If you've ever felt frustrated, overwhelmed, or unsure how to deal with your emotions, know this: You are not alone. And you have the power to grow, learn, and thrive. Keep this book close, return to it often, and embrace the journey of becoming the best version of yourself.

This book is not just a guide, it's a companion for the challenges and triumphs ahead.

- Melanie Cook, Certified Clinical Mental Health Counselor

ACKNOWLEDGMENTS: A HEARTFELT THANK YOU

Writing this book has been a wild, rewarding, and sometimes chaotic adventure, one that wouldn't have been possible without the incredible people who've supported me every step of the way.

To my family, my husband and children, thank you for being my greatest inspiration and my grounding force. Your love, laughter, and unwavering belief in me have pushed me forward, even when self-doubt tried to creep in. You are my reason, my motivation, and my biggest blessing.

To my parents, who left everything behind to build a better life in America. Your resilience, sacrifice, and work ethic have shaped every part of who I am today. Every dream I chase, every goal I accomplish, it's all because of the values you instilled in me.

To my mentors and business partners, thank you for challenging me, pushing me, and expanding my vision beyond what I ever thought possible. Your wisdom has been invaluable, and I am endlessly grateful for the lessons you've shared.

To my incredible team, the powerhouse individuals who help bring these ideas to life. You are the engine behind every success, the quiet force that keeps everything running smoothly. Your dedication, creativity, and relentless passion do not go unnoticed.

To my readers, followers, and supporters, whether you've been with me from the beginning or just picked up this book today, your encouragement fuels my passion. Seeing how these stories, lessons, and ideas impact your lives is the greatest reward I could ever ask for.

To my Collective for Children family, thank you for believing in the mission to empower every child with resilience, leadership, and emotional intelligence. Your commitment to making a difference is what drives me every day.

This book is not just mine, it is a product of so many incredible hearts and minds that have influenced, guided, and supported me along the way. I am forever grateful to each and every one of you.

With love and gratitude,
Mary Nhin

AUTHOR'S NOTE

Dear Reader,

When I was younger, I wished for a guidebook on emotions and feelings, a roadmap that could tell me why I felt the way I did and how to deal with it. Instead, I figured things out through trial and error, with plenty of stumbles along the way. Sometimes, I had the support of incredible people who lifted me up. Other times, I had to navigate things solo, learning as I went. Looking back, I wish I had a resource that not only explained emotions but also gave me real, practical ways to handle them.

That's exactly why I wrote this book, for you.

Whatever you're feeling, whether it's anger, sadness, anxiety, or self-doubt, know this: you are not alone. Emotions can be big, confusing, and overwhelming, but they're also incredibly powerful. They help shape who you are, deepen your connections with others, and push you to grow. Learning how to manage them isn't about shutting them down, it's about understanding them, working with them, and using them to your advantage.

This book? It's your companion. Keep it close. Flip to the chapters that hit home for you. Revisit the strategies when you need a little extra support. Emotions don't disappear overnight, but with practice, patience, and self-kindness, you'll notice yourself handling them with more confidence.

Every time you take a step toward understanding your emotions, you're becoming stronger, wiser, and more in control of your own story.

I believe in you. I hope this book helps you believe in yourself, too.

With love and support,
Mary Nhin

INTRODUCTION: MASTER YOUR EMOTIONS LIKE A NINJA!

Ever felt like your emotions were running the show, and you were just along for the ride? One moment you're laughing with friends, and the next, you're drowning in self-doubt. Yep, been there. That's why this book exists, to help you take back the driver's seat of your emotions.

Here's the truth, emotions aren't the enemy. They're a crucial part of being human, helping us navigate life, build connections, and figure out who we are. But knowing how to handle them without feeling overwhelmed? That's where the real challenge comes in. And guess what? It's totally possible.

That's exactly why I wrote this book. I want you to know that you're not alone. Everyone, kids, teens, even adults who pretend they have it all figured out, experiences big, messy emotions. The secret isn't in pushing them away, it's in learning how to work with them in a way that makes life easier, not harder. This book? It's your guide.

Inside, you'll find real-life stories, expert advice, and practical strategies to help you understand what's going on in your mind and body. Whether you're struggling with anger, stress, sadness, or self-confidence, you'll find tools to help you navigate tough moments and come out stronger on the other side.

This isn't just a book, it's your emotional toolkit. Keep it close. Flip to the chapters that resonate with you. Revisit the strategies when life gets overwhelming. And most importantly, remember this:

You are capable.

You are strong.
You have the power to shape your emotional well-being. I'm so glad you're here. Let's take on this journey together.

With love and support,
Mary Nhin

1

THE POWER OF KINDNESS

Kindness is like a superpower, one that doesn't require a cape, just a little heart. It has the ability to brighten someone's day, boost your own happiness, and even create a ripple effect that spreads beyond what you can see. The best part? You don't need to donate millions, perform grand gestures, or give away your last slice of pizza (unless you really want to). Tiny moments of kindness, holding the door, smiling, or giving someone a genuine compliment, are just as powerful.

And here's the wild thing, kindness is contagious. When someone experiences it, they're more likely to pass it on. Think about it: Ever had a stranger smile at you for no reason? That tiny act probably made you feel good, maybe even inspired you to be extra nice to the next person you saw.

One small act of kindness can lead to another, and another, until, BAM! The world is just a little bit brighter. One compliment, one high-five, one "Hey, I appreciate you" could be the spark that turns someone's day around. That's the magic of kindness, it doesn't just help others, it makes you feel great too.

Kindness in Action: Small Moves, Big Impact

You don't have to move mountains to make a difference. Sometimes, the tiniest gestures carry the most weight. A few simple ways to flex your kindness muscle include:

- Giving someone a genuine compliment (Not just "cool shoes," but "You have a great sense of style!")
- Helping a classmate who's struggling with homework (Bonus points if you do it without making them feel bad!)
- Letting someone go ahead of you in line (Yes, even if you really want that snack first.)
- Standing up for someone who's being left out (Because everyone deserves to feel included.)
- Listening without interrupting when someone needs to talk (Resisting the urge to chime in? That's peak ninja-level patience.)
- Sending a random "You got this!" text to a friend, just because (Trust me, they'll appreciate it.)

What Kindness Does to Your Brain and Body

Being kind isn't just good for others, it's good for you. Science says so. When you do something kind, your brain releases oxytocin (the feel-good hormone). This can:

- Make you feel warm and fuzzy inside
- Reduce stress and anxiety (kindness is basically nature's chill pill)
- Strengthen your connections with others (good vibes attract good people!)
- Boost your confidence and self-worth
- Basically, kindness is the ultimate win-win, helping others while making you feel awesome too.

The Art of Being Kind to Yourself

Here's the thing, kindness isn't just about how you treat others. It's also about how you treat yourself. Many people find it easy to be kind to their friends, family, or even strangers, but when it comes to themselves? Not so much.

Being kind to yourself means:

- Speaking to yourself like you would a friend (Would you call your friend a failure for messing up? No? Then don't do it to yourself.)
- Giving yourself permission to make mistakes and learn from them (Even if that mistake was spilling coffee on yourself twice in one day.)
- Taking care of your body with rest, good food, and movement (Your body works hard for you, treat it well!)
- Setting boundaries and saying 'no' when you need to (Because running yourself into the ground isn't kindness, it's exhaustion.)
- Forgiving yourself for past mistakes (Because everyone messes up sometimes.)

If you wouldn't say something cruel to a friend, why say it to yourself? Practicing self-kindness helps you build confidence, reduce stress, and create a more positive mindset. And when you're kind to yourself, you naturally have more kindness to share with the world.

So go ahead, be kind, to others, and to yourself. Because the world needs your good energy, and *so do you.*

Expert Advice

Dr. David Hamilton, a researcher on kindness, found that performing small acts of kindness strengthens the heart and immune system while reducing anxiety and depression.

Actionable Strategies

An Emotions Ninja follows the **G.I.F.T.** Method to spread kindness:

G – Give Without Expecting – Kindness is most powerful when given freely, not for attention or reward.
I – Include Others – Small gestures, like inviting someone to sit with you, can make people feel valued.
F – Find Opportunities – Look for ways to help, whether it's holding the door or offering a smile.
T – Take Time to Appreciate – Acknowledge acts of kindness from others and return the favor.

Other ways to practice kindness:

- Daily Gratitude: Write down three things you're thankful for each day.
- Kindness Challenge: Do one act of kindness each day and track how it makes you feel.
- Positive Affirmations: Compliment yourself and others genuinely and often.
- Try using these strategies and note how you feel.

Relatable Scenarios

Scenario 1: Standing Up for Someone Who Feels Left Out

You notice a classmate sitting alone at lunch, scrolling through their phone to look busy. Other students walk past without noticing. You think, *They probably feel uncomfortable.* You want to say something but hesitate, *What if they think it's weird?*

Choosing Kindness: Instead of overthinking, you walk over and invite them to sit with you. They seem surprised but smile and join in. Later, they tell you that your small act of kindness made their whole day. You realize that kindness doesn't have to be big, it just has to be intentional.

Scenario 2: Responding to Rudeness with Kindness

You're at the store when a stressed-out cashier snaps at you for no reason. Your first instinct is to snap back, but then you pause. *Maybe they're having a bad day.*

Choosing Kindness: Instead of taking it personally, you say something kind, like, *I hope your day gets better.* Their face softens, and they apologize. You walk away realizing that sometimes, people don't need more frustration, they need kindness to turn their day around.

Scenario 3: Helping Someone Who Doesn't Ask for It

A friend is struggling in class, but they don't want to ask for help. You hear them sighing as they look at their notes, frustrated. You could ignore it, or you could offer to help.

Choosing Kindness: You lean over and say, *Hey, I struggled with this too, but I found a trick that helped.* They light up and ask you to explain. By sharing what you know, you make learning easier for both of you, and show that kindness means looking out for others, even when they don't ask.

Scenario 4: Choosing Encouragement Instead of Criticism

Your friend posts a drawing they made on social media. It's not perfect, and people leave some harsh comments. You see it and think, *They worked hard on this. They don't deserve this negativity.*

Choosing Kindness: Instead of ignoring it, you leave a positive comment: *This is amazing! I can see how much effort you put into it.* Your friend texts you later, saying your support meant a lot. You realize that kindness has the power to build someone up, even when the world tries to tear them down.

"**No** act of kindness, no matter how small, is ever wasted." – AESOP

Personal Story: The Power of Belief and Kindness

When I was in first grade, English felt like an unsolved mystery, a puzzle with too many pieces and no clear picture. My family spoke another language at home, and while other kids breezed through books, I felt like I was running a race with my shoelaces tied together.

I'd sit in class, watching my classmates raise their hands with confidence, their words flowing effortlessly while I shrank in my seat, afraid to speak up. The words on the page blurred together, and every time I stumbled, embarrassment crept in, whispering, *Maybe you'll never catch up.*

But then, Mrs. Ruth Payne entered the picture, my real-life superhero in a cardigan. She didn't see a struggling student. She saw potential. Instead of letting me fall behind, she went out of her way to help me. After school, while my classmates ran off to play or head home, Mrs. Payne sat with me, patiently guiding me through my lessons, never rushing, never making me feel less-than.

She didn't just teach me English, she taught me belief. She made learning feel less like an obstacle course and more like an adventure. Little by little, I improved. By second grade, not only had I caught up, I had skipped a reading level.

Looking back, I realize that Mrs. Payne's kindness didn't just help me academically, it changed the course of my life. She proved that one person's belief in you can be the spark that ignites self-confidence. Because of her, I learned that learning isn't something to fear, it's something to embrace.

That lesson stayed with me. It's one of the reasons I wanted to become a teacher myself and why I prioritize educators today. Kindness isn't just about being nice, it's about unlocking potential, believing in others when they can't yet see their own strengths.

Because of Mrs. Payne, I learned to believe in myself. And now, I strive to pass that same kindness forward, knowing that one small act of encouragement can create ripples that last a lifetime.

Ninja Wisdom

Kindness isn't a weakness, it's a strength that has the power to change the world.

Case Study: The Cafeteria Challenge

Jamal was having the worst day. His backpack strap had broken, his phone was at 2% battery, and the vending machine ate his dollar. But the final straw? Seeing Mia sitting alone in the cafeteria, staring at her tray. He hesitated, what if she didn't want company? But then, he thought about how he'd feel in her place. Taking a deep breath, he walked over and sat down. "You okay?" he asked. Mia looked surprised but then smiled. "Yeah, just a long day." They talked about their favorite shows, and by the end of lunch, Jamal realized something, kindness wasn't just about helping others; it made him feel better too.

Quick Quiz Box

> **Which of the following is an example of kindness?**
>
> - a) Holding the door for someone
> - b) Ignoring someone struggling
> - c) Making fun of someone
> - d) Only being kind when it benefits you

(Answer: a) Holding the door for someone)

Journal Reflection Box

Write about a time when someone was kind to you. How did it make you feel? How can you pass that kindness on?

Action Challenge Chart

Kindness Opportunity	Action	How It Made Me Feel
A friend is upset	Send them an encouraging text	Warm and connected
Someone drops their books	Help pick them up	Helpful and positive
New student at school	Invite them to sit with you	Inclusive and friendly

By taking small, intentional steps toward kindness, like the ones in the Action Challenge Chart, you can experience firsthand how simple acts make a big difference. Now, let's reflect on the key takeaways from this chapter.

Chapter 1 Key Takeaways

Kindness is contagious, one small act can inspire a ripple effect. Self-kindness is just as important as kindness toward others. Thoughtful gestures, even tiny ones, can have a big impact.

Mini-FAQ

Q1: What if I'm kind, but people don't appreciate it?
A: Kindness isn't about getting something in return. Focus on how it makes you feel and trust that positivity spreads.

Q2: Can I be too kind?
A: Kindness should never mean ignoring your own needs. Balance kindness with healthy boundaries!

Kindness can help build strong relationships, but what happens when anger takes over? In the next chapter, we'll learn how to recognize and manage anger before it controls you.

THE POWER OF KINDNESS

2

MANAGING ANGER BEFORE IT MANAGES YOU

Anger is like a fire-breathing dragon, it can either burn everything down or be tamed into a powerful force for good. If left unchecked, it can lead to regretful decisions, broken relationships, and stress levels so high you'd think you just ran a marathon (without the fitness benefits). But here's the secret: anger itself isn't bad, it's how we express and control it that matters. When you learn to manage anger, you can prevent outbursts, improve communication, and handle conflicts like a true ninja, swift, sharp, and totally in control.

Actually, anger can be useful. It helps us stand up for ourselves, push through challenges, and make important changes. In some situations, anger is like an internal alarm system, alerting us when something feels unfair or when boundaries have been crossed. It can motivate us to take action, whether that means speaking up, setting boundaries, or advocating for change.

But, and this is a BIG but, when anger isn't managed well, it can get messy. Picture a soda bottle being shaken and then exploding all over the place. (Yeah, that messy.) It can make us say things we don't mean, damage relationships, and lead to choices we regret. Holding it all in isn't much better, it just turns into stress, anxiety, and even physical issues like headaches, high blood pressure, or trouble sleeping. So, instead of bottling it up or exploding like a volcano, let's talk about how to channel that fiery energy into something positive.

The Different Types of Anger

Not all anger looks the same. Understanding the different forms it can take can help us recognize and manage it more effectively:

1. Passive Anger – This is when anger is hidden, like a ninja lurking in the shadows. It shows up as sarcasm, avoidance, or silent resentment. (Ever given someone the silent treatment? Yeah, that's passive anger.)
2. Aggressive Anger – This is the Hulk smash kind of anger. Yelling, blaming, throwing things, or physically lashing out, it's like setting off an emotional fireworks display (but way less fun).
3. Assertive Anger – This is anger handled like a pro. It means expressing feelings calmly, setting boundaries, and working toward solutions. This is the real ninja move, taking control without losing control.

The Sneaky Consequences of Uncontrolled Anger

If anger isn't managed properly, it can cause more problems than it solves:

- Damaged Relationships – No one likes being on the receiving end of an outburst, and constant anger can push people away.
- Poor Decision-Making – Acting on anger without thinking can lead to impulsive choices (like rage-texting, which never ends well).
- Increased Stress & Anxiety – Anger triggers the body's stress response, and when it happens too often, it can take a toll on your mental health.

- Negative Self-Perception – If anger makes you say or do things you regret, it can lead to guilt and lower self-esteem.

Why Managing Anger is Your Superpower

Learning how to handle anger is one of the best life skills you can master. It helps you:
1. Stay calm under pressure
2. Strengthen relationships instead of damaging them
3. Communicate effectively (instead of yelling like a cartoon villain)
4. Turn anger into action, advocating for yourself and making positive changes

Anger isn't the enemy, it's what we do with it that matters. And you, my friend, have the power to turn that energy into something incredible. So, let's talk about how to spot anger before it takes over.

What Anger Feels Like in the Body

When anger rises, your body goes into fight-or-flight mode, basically, your brain thinks you're in an action movie chase scene. The heart beats faster, muscles tense up, and breathing becomes shallow. Some people feel like they're going to explode, while others hold it all in and let frustration simmer like an over boiling pot.

Signs of Anger in the Body

- Tense muscles and clenched fists
- Racing heartbeat and flushed face
- Shallow, quick breathing
- The urge to yell, storm away, or throw something dramatically (resist the urge, your phone does not deserve this)

The key is noticing these signs early so you can regain control before anger escalates. Think of it like catching a leak before it floods the entire house.

So, the next time you feel that fire building inside, take a deep breath, step back, and remember, you're in control of your reaction, not the other way around.

Expert Advice: How to Keep Anger from Running the Show

Dr. Raymond Novaco, a leading psychologist in anger management, explains that anger itself isn't the problem, it's how we react to it that matters. Anger is a natural emotion (yes, even that "WHY IS THIS WIFI SO SLOW" kind of anger), but when we let it take control, that's when things get messy.

Actionable Strategies

An Emotions Ninja uses the **1 + 3 + 10** method to handle anger effectively:

1. Say 1 calm word like "Relax" or "Breathe."
2. Take 3 deep breaths to slow down your emotions.
3. Count to 10 before responding.

Sometimes, there is not a one size fits all strategy. Other effective anger management strategies include:

- Journaling emotions instead of reacting impulsively.
- Stepping away from the situation until feeling calmer.
- Practicing physical movement like running or punching a pillow to release built-up energy.

Try these the next time anger starts bubbling up and see how they help you respond rather than react. There may be one here that can help you tremendously to calm down.

Relatable Teen Scenarios

Scenario 1: Frustration in Sports

You're playing in an important basketball game, and your team is one point away from winning. You take the final shot… and miss. Your teammates sigh in frustration, and you feel your face heat up. *Why did I mess up? I let everyone down!*

    Making the Wise Choice: You feel the urge to yell or storm off the court. But then, you take a deep breath and remind yourself: *Even the best players miss shots sometimes. I'll learn from this and keep practicing.*

Scenario 2: A Sibling Takes Your Stuff

Your younger sibling sneaks into your room (again) and takes your favorite hoodie without asking. You find it crumpled on the floor, and before you know it, your hands are clenched into fists. *They never respect my space!*

    Making the Wise Choice: You want to yell, but instead, you walk away and cool off before talking to them. Later, you calmly explain why you're upset and set a boundary. *Next time, just ask before borrowing my things.*

Scenario 3: Unfair Blame at School

You're in class, working quietly, when the teacher suddenly calls you out for talking, even though it was your friend whispering next to you. Embarrassment turns into anger. *That's not fair! I wasn't even talking!*

    Making the Wise Choice: You want to argue, but instead, you take a deep breath and wait for a better moment to explain. Later, after class, you respectfully tell your teacher what happened, and they apologize for the mistake.

Scenario 4: A Friend Cancels Plans Last Minute

You've been looking forward to hanging out with your best friend all week. You've made plans, picked a movie, and even saved your allowance for snacks. Then, they text: *Sorry, can't make it.* No explanation. You feel hurt and annoyed, you could have made other plans!

Making the Wise Choice: Before reacting, you remind yourself: Maybe something came up. Instead of sending an angry text, you check in: *Hey, is everything okay? I was really looking forward to today.*

"**Holding** on to anger is like drinking poison and expecting the other person to die." — Buddha

Personal Story: The Rumor That Almost Broke Me

When I was younger, I learned the hard way that rumors have a way of spreading faster than a viral TikTok dance. One day, everything was fine, normal, even. The next? People were whispering behind my back, side-eyeing me in the hallways, and treating me like I'd just been voted Most Suspicious Person of the Year.

At first, I laughed it off. *A rumor? About me? That's ridiculous.* But as the whispers turned into actual conversations, I felt my anger bubbling up. *Who started this? Why are people believing it? And how do I make it stop?!*

My first instinct? Go full detective mode and call out the person responsible. But after taking a few deep breaths (and maybe eating an emergency snack), I decided on a different approach. Instead of reacting out of anger, I waited and observed. I wanted to see if confronting it head-on was even worth it.

Turns out, time did the work for me. Within a week, the rumor had lost its power, replaced by the next big drama. And me? I realized that sometimes, the best response is no response at all.

Lesson learned: Anger can be a knee-jerk reaction, but it doesn't always lead to the outcome you want. Instead of letting emotions dictate my next move, I chose to think strategically, *and it paid off.*

Ninja Wisdom

Anger is normal. It's how you handle it that makes a difference.

Case Study: The Soccer Meltdown

Jordan was known for his speed, but after missing a crucial goal, his temper took over. He kicked the turf so hard he almost launched his shoe into orbit. "I quit!" he yelled. His coach pulled him aside. "You can be mad, or you can get better, your choice." Jordan took a deep breath, practiced more, and in the next game, he scored the winning goal. He realized anger didn't have to control him, it could fuel his determination (preferably without footwear incidents).

Quick Quiz Box

> **When you feel angry, what is the first thing you should do?**
>
> - a) React immediately
> - b) Take deep breaths
> - c) Yell at someone
> - d) Ignore it completely

(Answer: b) Take deep breaths)

Journal Reflection Box

Write about a time when you felt really angry. What triggered it? How did you react? Looking back, would you handle it differently?

Action Challenge Chart

Situation	Initial Reaction	Alternative Response Using 1+3+10
Losing a game	Throwing the controller	Saying a calming phrase like "It's okay"
Argument with a friend	Yelling and blaming	Counting to 10 and talking calmly
Frustrated with homework	Slamming books shut	Taking deep breaths and trying again or asking for help

Managing frustration in the moment can be challenging, but using strategies like 1+3+10 can help turn impulsive reactions into thoughtful responses. Now, let's review the key takeaways from this chapter.

Chapter 2 Takeaways

- Anger is a natural emotion, but how you handle it makes all the difference.
- Cooling down before reacting leads to better decisions and stronger relationships.
- Expressing anger in a healthy way prevents regretful outbursts.

Mini-FAQ

Q1: What if I get angry too quickly?
A: Try the 1 + 3 + 10 Rule, say one calming word, take three deep breaths, and count to ten before responding. It gives your brain

time to think first.

Q2: Is bottling up anger better than expressing it?
A: No! Suppressed anger builds up and can explode later. Find healthy ways to let it out, like journaling, exercising, or talking it out.

Now that you know how to manage anger, let's dive deeper into how your thoughts, feelings, and behaviors are connected. In the next chapter, we'll explore the power of the CBT Triangle.

3

UNDERSTANDING THE CONNECTION BETWEEN THOUGHTS, FEELINGS, AND BEHAVIORS

Here's the truth: your thoughts love to play tricks on you. They act like they're the ultimate truth-tellers, but sometimes? They're straight-up liars. Once you realize that not every thought you have is 100% accurate, you gain the power to rewrite the story in your head, and that changes everything.

Negative thoughts can feel so real in the moment. One bad grade? *I'll never be smart enough.* A disagreement with a friend? *Nobody likes me.* Mess up a presentation? *I'm a total failure.* These thoughts spiral out of control faster than a dropped ice cream cone on a summer day, but here's the thing: just because you think it, doesn't make it true.

Meet CBT: The Thought Trainer

Cognitive Behavioral Therapy (CBT) is based on one powerful idea: your thoughts, feelings, and actions are all connected. Dr. Aaron Beck, the founder of CBT, discovered that the way we think about a situation influences how we feel, which then impacts how we act.

Change your thoughts, and you change your emotions. Change your emotions, and you change your actions. Boom. Mind blown.

That means instead of letting negative thoughts run the show, you can take back control. This chapter will introduce you to the CBT Triangle, a game-changing tool that helps break free from negative cycles and put you back in charge of your emotions. Because let's be real, you deserve to be the main character in your own story, not just a bystander to your anxious brain's over-dramatic plot twists.

Your brain's main job is to keep you safe, which means it's always scanning for potential problems. The downside? Sometimes it overdoes it, convincing you that a single mistake = total disaster. But here's the thing: The problem isn't having negative thoughts, it's believing them without questioning them.

The Cycle of Thoughts, Feelings, and Behaviors

Imagine this: You have a big presentation coming up. Here's how things can go two very different ways:

The Negative Thought Spiral

1. A thought appears: I don't think I can do this presentation.
2. That thought leads to a feeling: Anxiety kicks in, your palms sweat, your heart races.
3. Your feelings influence your behavior: Instead of practicing, you avoid preparing, which makes you even more nervous. The result? A total confidence meltdown.

The Confidence Loop

1. *A thought appears: This presentation is scary, but I can prepare and do my best.*
2. *That thought leads to a feeling:* You're still nervous (totally normal), but now you're also feeling determined.

3. *Your feelings influence your behavior:* You practice, prepare, and by the time you step up to speak, you're way more confident than you expected.

The key? Challenging negative thoughts and replacing them with ones that actually help you. Because let's be real, would you talk to your best friend the way your brain sometimes talks to you? No? Then it's time to start treating yourself with that same kindness.

Expert Advice

Dr. David Burns, author of Feeling Good: The New Mood Therapy, found that writing down negative thoughts and replacing them with rational ones can significantly improve mood.

Actionable Strategies

An Emotions Ninja uses the **CBT Triangle** to break free from negative thought patterns:

- **Thoughts**: Recognize negative thoughts when they appear.
- **Feelings**: Identify how those thoughts make you feel.
- **Behaviors**: Change your response by shifting your mindset.

Examples of Challenging Negative Thoughts

Negative Thought	Reframed Thought
"I'll never be good at this."	"I can improve with practice."
"Nobody likes me."	"I have people who care about me."
"If I fail, it's over."	"Mistakes help me grow."

Other techniques to rewire your thinking:

- Thought Journaling: Write down negative thoughts and challenge them with evidence.
- Reality Checks: Ask yourself, *Is this thought really true? What's another way to look at this?*
- Gratitude Practice: Focusing on the positives helps rewire your brain for optimism.
- Mindfulness and Meditation: Being present helps you detach from unhelpful thoughts. Mindfulness is the practice of being fully present and aware in the moment, without judgment. It involves focusing on your thoughts, emotions, and surroundings with curiosity and acceptance rather than reacting impulsively or getting overwhelmed.

Try these strategies the next time you have negative thoughts!

Relatable Scenarios for Teens

Scenario 1: You send a text to your friend, and they don't reply right away. Your mind immediately jumps to They must be mad at me. You start to feel anxious and decide to avoid them at school the next day. Later, you find out they were just busy with homework.

Reframing the Thought: If you had challenged the thought earlier, you could have saved yourself a lot of stress.

Scenario 2: You get a bad grade on a test. Instead of thinking, I can study differently next time, your mind goes straight to I'm terrible at this subject. I'll never be good at it. Because of this, you stop putting in effort, making it even harder to improve.

Reframing the Thought: But what if you told yourself, This is just one test. I can learn from my mistakes. That small shift in thinking could completely change how you approach learning.

"**Whether** you think you can or think you can't, you're right." — Henry Ford

Personal Story: The Math Meltdown That Changed Everything

Math and I have had a complicated relationship, kind of like a bad rom-com where one person (me) tries really hard, and the other (math) just isn't interested. No matter how much effort I put in, math refused to love me back.

Then came the big test. The one I actually studied for. The one that was supposed to prove I had finally cracked the code.
I sat down, cracked my knuckles, and flipped over the test paper, ready to dominate. And then,
Immediate. Full. Panic.

The numbers on the page looked like they were written in ancient hieroglyphics. My brain went into full-blown DEFCON 1. *I'm terrible at math. I'm going to fail. If I fail, my grade will tank. If my grade tanks, I won't get into college. If I don't get into college, I'll end up living in my parents' basement forever, eating cold pizza and talking to my pet goldfish about missed opportunities.*

Cue internal freak-out.

My heart pounded. My palms got sweaty (knees weak, arms heavy, Eminem gets it). I tried to focus, but my brain had already written my academic obituary. I barely finished the test, convinced that my doom was sealed.

But then, plot twist, I didn't fail.

I didn't ace it either, but I did way better than my anxiety had predicted. And that's when it hit me: I hadn't actually bombed the test. I had bombed my own confidence.

Thankfully, my teacher saw what was happening. She pulled me aside and introduced me to CBT (Cognitive Behavioral Therapy) techniques. She explained something that completely flipped my perspective:

Thoughts aren't facts. Just because my brain was screaming *I'm going to fail* didn't mean it was true.

She challenged me to reframe my thinking: *What if I'm not*

actually bad at math? What if I just need to practice differently?

At first, I was skeptical. My brain had been my personal roast master for years, was I really supposed to start questioning it now? But I gave it a shot. Instead of assuming failure, I started treating tests as challenges instead of death sentences. I stopped labeling myself as "bad at math" and started focusing on where I could improve.

The result? Game changer.

Over time, I stopped spiraling every time I saw a math problem. I still wasn't Einstein, but I got better at managing my emotions and actually *learning* instead of letting anxiety take the wheel. And that? That was the biggest win of all.

Lesson learned: Your thoughts will try to trick you. Don't believe everything your brain tells you, especially when it's predicting disaster. Challenge it, question it, and reframe it, because sometimes, you're way more capable than you think you are.

Ninja Wisdom

Your thoughts shape your reality. When you change the way you think, you change the way you experience life.

Case Study: The Pop Quiz Panic

Samantha stared at the surprise quiz in front of her. *I'm going to fail. I always fail at math.* Her hands started sweating. Then, she remembered what her teacher said about thoughts affecting emotions. *Wait, I studied for this. I know more than I think.* She took a deep breath, changed her mindset, and ended up scoring better than expected.

Quick Quiz Box

What is the main idea of CBT?

- a) Our thoughts, feelings, and behaviors are connected
- b) Only feelings determine our actions
- c) Changing thoughts doesn't affect emotions
- d) Ignoring emotions makes them go away

(Answer: a) Our thoughts, feelings, and behaviors are connected)

Journal Reflection Box

Write about a recent negative thought you had. How did it affect your feelings and actions? How could you reframe it next time?

Action Challenge Chart

Thought Pattern	Initial Reaction	A Healthier Response
"I'm not good at this."	Giving up	Trying again with a growth mindset
"Everyone is judging me."	Avoiding situations	Reminding myself that people are focused on themselves
"This will never get better."	Feeling hopeless	Taking small steps toward improvement

Recognizing and reshaping negative thoughts can transform the way you feel and respond to challenges. Now, let's explore the key takeaways from this chapter.

Chapter 3 Key Takeaways

- Your thoughts shape how you feel, changing one can change them all.
- Negative thoughts aren't always true, challenge and reframe them.
- Small mindset shifts lead to big emotional improvements over time.

Mini-FAQ

Q1: What if I can't stop negative thoughts?
A: Thoughts are habits, practice reframing them daily to train your brain toward more helpful thinking.

Q2: Can I completely stop negative thinking?
A: No one has 100% positive thoughts all the time! The goal is to

challenge negative ones so they don't control you.

Our thoughts can shape our reality, but they can also create worry and fear. In the next chapter, we'll tackle anxiety and discover strategies to stay calm and in control.

4

MANAGING ANXIETY

Anxiety is like that one friend who means well, but takes things way too far. It's your brain's way of trying to keep you safe, like a built-in alarm system. But sometimes, instead of just warning you about actual danger (like a bear chasing you, which, let's be honest, isn't likely), it freaks out over things like *a pop quiz, talking to someone new, or saying something awkward two years ago that no one even remembers.*

The truth is, everyone experiences anxiety in some way. It can show up as nervousness before a test, worry about the future, or fear of embarrassing yourself in front of others. In small doses, anxiety is actually helpful, it keeps you alert and prepared. But when it sticks around too long, it starts feeling like you're carrying a backpack full of bricks everywhere you go. Heavy, exhausting, and impossible to ignore.

A lot of teens struggle with anxiety but don't always know how to talk about it. It can feel like a storm in your mind, thoughts spinning out of control, heart pounding, muscles tensing up, making you feel like you're about to *implode*. But here's the most important thing to know: Anxiety doesn't define you, and you are not alone.

It's a skill to learn how to manage it, just like learning how to ride a bike or solve a tricky math problem. And the best part? It gets easier with practice.

Different Types of Anxiety, Which One Sounds Familiar?

Anxiety isn't one-size-fits-all. It comes in different shapes, sizes, and *flavors of overthinking*. Here are some common ones:

1. Generalized Anxiety – The "worry about everything" mode, grades, friendships, the future, even when there's no real reason to stress.
2. Social Anxiety – The fear of being judged or embarrassed, like speaking in class or walking into a room full of people and feeling like all eyes are on you (spoiler: they're not).
3. Performance Anxiety – The pressure to be perfect in academics, sports, or activities, leading to stress and self-doubt. (Because obviously, the world is watching your every move… except, it's not.)
4. Test Anxiety – The "brain goes blank" syndrome, you studied, but the moment the test starts, your mind is suddenly *a static TV screen*.
5. Separation Anxiety – Feeling uneasy when away from home, family, or a familiar place, even if it's just for a little while.
6. Health Anxiety – Constantly worrying about getting sick or something bad happening to your health, even when there are no actual symptoms.

Step one in managing anxiety? Figuring out which kind you're dealing with. When you name it, you can tame it.

What Anxiety Feels Like in the Body

Anxiety isn't just in your head, it's a full-body experience. Your brain sends a distress signal to your nervous system, triggering fight, flight, or freeze mode, even if the only "danger" is giving a presentation. (Which, to be fair, can feel like staring down a hungry lion.)

Common Physical Symptoms of Anxiety

» Racing heart & shallow breathing – Your body's way of saying, *"Ready to run?"* (Even if there's nowhere to run.)

» Sweaty palms & shaky hands – As if you're about to arm wrestle a professional weightlifter.

» Restless thoughts & overthinking – Every worst-case scenario playing in your mind like a never-ending movie trailer.

» Tightness in the chest or stomach aches – Your body's way of telling you it's stressed… in the most dramatic way possible.

» Feeling dizzy, lightheaded, or frozen in place – Your body panics so hard, it forgets what to do.

» Trouble sleeping & constant worrying – Because why not replay embarrassing moments from three years ago *at 2 AM?*

The good news? Recognizing these signs early is the first step to taking control. Anxiety might try to boss you around, but guess what? You're the one in charge. And this chapter is here to show you how to take that power back.

Expert Advice

Dr. Lisa Damour, a psychologist specializing in teen anxiety, explains that anxiety is often a sign of growth, it happens when we step outside our comfort zone. Instead of avoiding what makes us anxious, she suggests slowly facing those fears to build confidence.

Actionable Strategies

An Emotions Ninja uses the **Three Rs Method** to stop anxious thoughts from spiraling out of control:

- **Recognize** – Notice when anxiety starts to build up. Pay attention to the thoughts racing through your mind and the physical sensations in your body.
- **Relax** – Use grounding techniques like deep breathing, stretching, or squeezing a stress ball. This helps calm your nervous system.
- **Refocus** – Challenge anxious thoughts with logic. Ask yourself: Is this fear based on facts, or is my brain exaggerating? Shift your focus to what you can control.

Other helpful techniques include:

- Box Breathing: Inhale for four seconds, hold for four, exhale for four, hold again for four. Repeat until you feel calmer.
- 5-4-3-2-1 Grounding: Name five things you can see, four things you can touch, three things you hear, two things you smell, and one thing you taste. This brings your focus back to the present.
- Reframing Your Thoughts: Instead of thinking, *What if I fail?*, try thinking, *What if I do great?*

Try incorporating these calming activities the next time you feel anxious!

Relatable Teen Scenarios

Scenario 1: Social Anxiety

You're about to walk into a crowded lunchroom when suddenly, your stomach drops. *What if I don't have anyone to sit with? What if people judge me?* Your hands get sweaty, and you feel like turning around and eating in the bathroom instead.

Reframing the Thought: *Maybe people are too busy with their own friends to notice me. I'll take a deep breath and find a friendly face.*

Scenario 2: Test Anxiety

You've studied for your math test all week, but as soon as you sit down, your mind goes blank. Your heart races, your palms sweat, and you can't focus on the questions.

Reframing the Thought: *I've studied and prepared for this. I'll start with the questions I know and take deep breaths to stay calm.*

Scenario 3: Performance Anxiety

You're next in line to present in front of the class. Your legs feel like jelly, and your mind keeps repeating, *What if I forget my lines? What if everyone laughs?*

Reframing the Thought: *Feeling nervous means I care about doing well. I'll take a deep breath and speak slowly, one sentence at a time.*

By learning to recognize and challenge anxious thoughts, you can break free from the cycle of fear and self-doubt.

"**Anxiety** does not empty tomorrow of its sorrows, but only empties today of its strength."
— Charles Spurgeon

Personal Story: My Battle with the Dreaded Presentation

Public speaking. Two words that struck pure terror into my high school soul. The night before my big presentation, my brain went into full-on disaster mode: *What if I mess up? What if everyone laughs? What if I forget everything and just stand there like a malfunctioning robot?!* The more I thought about it, the worse I felt.

By bedtime, my stomach was doing Olympic-level gymnastics, my palms were sweaty enough to water a plant, and my heart was pounding like a drum solo at a rock concert. Sleep? Ha. Not happening.

The next morning, I was desperate. I pulled out my best excuse and told my teacher I wasn't feeling well, *hoping* she'd let me off the hook. But instead of excusing me, she sat down and said something that completely changed my mindset:

"Anxiety is like a wave. If you fight against it, it feels stronger. But if you let yourself ride it, it eventually calms down."

Huh. That was new.

Then she taught me a simple breathing technique, inhale for four seconds, hold for four, exhale for four. I figured, *Why not?* I tried it, and slowly, the storm inside my chest started to settle.

When it was finally time to present, I was still nervous, but something had shifted. Instead of seeing fear as a sign of failure, I realized it was just a sign that I cared. So I focused on one sentence at a time, reminding myself that I didn't need to be perfect, I just needed to keep going.

And then? Before I knew it, I was done.

That experience changed everything for me. I learned that fear doesn't mean failure, it means growth. Anxiety might still show up uninvited, but it doesn't have to run the show. Now, whenever I feel those nerves creeping in, I remember: *Ride the wave, don't fight it.*

Ninja Wisdom

Anxiety is like a storm, it feels powerful, but it always passes. When you learn to ride the waves of anxiety instead of fighting them, you gain control over your emotions and your future.

Case Study: The Stage Fright Incident

Leo loved playing guitar but hated performing. Before the talent show, his mind raced: What if I mess up? What if everyone laughs? His mom reminded him to take deep breaths and picture success. On stage, he stumbled at first but kept going. The audience cheered, and he realized his anxiety wasn't as powerful as his love for music.

Quick Quiz Box

Which of the following is the best way to manage anxiety?

- a) Take deep breaths and focus on the present
- b) Avoid anything that makes you anxious
- c) Keep worrying until the situation is over
- d) Ignore your feelings and push them away

(Answer: a) Take deep breaths and focus on the present)

Journal Reflection Box

Write about a time when you felt anxious. What were your thoughts? How did you handle it? What could you do differently next time?

Action Challenge Chart

Anxiety Trigger	Initial Reaction	A Healthier Response
Speaking in class	Feeling frozen	Relax with deep breaths
Meeting new people	Avoiding conversation	Recognizing when you start to feel anxious and relax with deep breaths
Big test coming up	Overthinking and panicking	Refocus with positive self-talk

Try these strategies the next time anxiety creeps in!

Chapter 4 Key Takeaways

- Anxiety is your brain's way of trying to protect you, but it can become overwhelming.
- Breathing and grounding techniques help regain control in anxious moments.
- Focusing on what you can control helps reduce unnecessary worry.

Mini-FAQ

Q1: What if my anxiety feels too big to handle?
A: Break it down. Use the 3 Rs, Recognize, Relax, Refocus, to regain control, one step at a time.

Q2: Does anxiety ever go away completely?
A: Anxiety will always be a part of life, but you can learn to manage it so it doesn't control you.

Anxiety can feel overwhelming, but understanding it is a big step toward emotional strength. Now, let's switch gears and explore happiness, what it really is and how you can create more of it in your life.

5

UNLOCKING THE SCIENCE OF HAPPINESS

Let's talk about happiness, the thing we're all chasing but sometimes feel like we'll never quite catch. It's easy to think happiness is something that just happens, like winning the lottery, waking up with perfect hair, or discovering that your favorite snack is suddenly on sale. But here's the truth: happiness isn't something you wait for, it's something you create.

Many people believe happiness comes from external factors, having the right friends, getting straight A's, landing the lead role in the school play, or finally hitting that perfect TikTok dance on the first try. While these things can bring joy, they're not the foundation of lasting happiness. Research in positive psychology shows that external circumstances only account for about 10% of our happiness. That's right, just 10%! The other 90% comes from our mindset, habits, and the way we choose to respond to life.

Translation? You have way more control over your happiness than you think.

Happiness isn't about luck or waiting for "one day" when life is finally perfect. It's about small, intentional habits, things you can start doing today to train your brain to feel happier and more fulfilled right now.

The Science Behind Happiness: Your Daily D.O.S.E.

Scientists have figured out that happiness is closely linked to four key brain chemicals, Dopamine, Oxytocin, Serotonin, and Endorphins. (Or as I like to call it, your Daily D.O.S.E. of happiness.) When you engage in activities that release these chemicals, your mood improves, your stress decreases, and life just feels better.

- Dopamine (The Motivation Molecule) – Released when you achieve a goal or experience success. This is your "I did it!" feeling that makes you want to keep going. Think: finishing an assignment, scoring a goal, or even checking something off your to-do list.
- Oxytocin (The Connection Chemical) – Released through social bonding, hugs, and acts of kindness. It's the reason why spending time with loved ones, petting a dog, or even giving someone a heartfelt compliment makes you feel warm and fuzzy inside.
- Serotonin (The Mood Stabilizer) – Helps regulate emotions and is boosted by things like gratitude, positive memories, and spending time in nature. Ever feel amazing after sitting outside in the sun or reflecting on something good? That's serotonin at work!
- Endorphins (The Natural Stress-Reliever) – These reduce pain and boost pleasure and are released through exercise, laughter, and music. That "runner's high" after a workout? The uncontrollable giggles during a funny movie? Yep, that's endorphins in action.

The best part? You don't have to wait for happiness to show up, you can actively trigger these chemicals every single day by doing small, intentional things that make you feel good.

How to Cultivate Happiness From Within

The good news? Happiness is a skill, not just an emotion. And just like any skill, the more you practice, the stronger it gets. Here's how you can boost your happiness levels every single day:

- Shift Your Mindset – Your brain is a powerful filter. If you focus on what's missing, life will always feel lacking. But if you train your brain to see the good in everyday moments, happiness becomes second nature. Practicing gratitude, celebrating small wins, and choosing to focus on the positives can rewire your brain to be happier.
- Engage in Meaningful Activities – True happiness isn't just about having fun; it's about feeling engaged and fulfilled. Doing things that challenge you, reading, learning, creating, helping others, brings deeper satisfaction than just scrolling on your phone for hours (even if the memes are great).
- Build Positive Relationships – Surround yourself with people who uplift and support you. The company you keep has a huge impact on your happiness. Find friends who bring out the best in you, and be that friend for someone else.
- Take Care of Your Mind and Body – Your physical health and mental health are besties. Getting enough sleep, eating nutritious foods, and moving your body all play a big role in how you feel emotionally. A healthy body makes it easier to have a healthy mind.
- Let Go of Comparisons – The fastest way to steal your own happiness? Comparing yourself to others. Social media makes this ridiculously easy, but remember: it's a highlight reel, not real life. Instead of measuring your life against someone else's, focus on your own progress, growth, and unique journey.

Take Control of Your Happiness

Happiness isn't something you stumble upon, it's something you create. When you understand that it comes from your mindset, daily habits, and the way you engage with life, you take control of your own emotional well-being. Instead of saying, I'll be happy when…, you start realizing, I can be happy now. So, don't wait for happiness to magically appear. Start building it today. One small habit, one shift in perspective, one positive action at a time. Because happiness isn't a destination, it's a way of traveling.

What Happiness Feels Like in the Body

Happiness isn't just an emotion, it's a state of mind and a physical response in the body.

- Light, energetic, and motivated
- Relaxed and calm, with a sense of peace
- Feeling connected to others and engaged in activities
- Positive and hopeful thoughts about the future
- A boost in energy levels and creativity

Expert Advice

Dr. Laurie Santos, a happiness researcher at Yale, discovered that happiness isn't about external success, it's about daily habits like gratitude, mindfulness, and social connection.

Actionable Strategies

An Emotions Ninja follows the **Daily D.O.S.E. Method**, a scientifically backed way to boost happiness:

D – Dopamine: The motivation and reward chemical. You can boost it by:

» Setting small, achievable goals and celebrating wins
» Exercising or engaging in physical activity
» Learning something new or solving puzzles

O – Oxytocin: The connection and bonding chemical. You can boost it by:

- » Hugging friends or family
- » Spending quality time with loved ones
- » Performing acts of kindness or giving compliments

S – Serotonin: The mood stabilizer. You can boost it by:

- » Getting sunlight and spending time outside
- » Practicing gratitude and thinking about positive memories
- » Eating nutritious foods that support brain health

E – Endorphins: The body's natural painkillers and stress relievers. You can boost them by:

- » Laughing and watching something funny
- » Listening to your favorite music
- » Engaging in creative activities like drawing, writing, or playing an instrument

Try incorporating these happiness-boosting activities into your daily routine and notice how they impact your mood and mindset!

In addition to the **Daily D.O.S.E.** method, here are other proven ways to cultivate happiness:

- Mindfulness and Meditation: Taking a few minutes each day to focus on your breath and surroundings can help reduce stress and improve overall happiness.
- Acts of Kindness: Doing something nice for someone else, whether it's writing a kind note, helping a friend, or volunteering, can create lasting joy.

- Limiting Screen Time: Too much social media can contribute to comparison and negativity. Taking breaks and spending time offline can improve mental well-being.
- Journaling: Writing down your thoughts, feelings, or even simple gratitude lists can help reframe your mindset toward positivity.
- Getting Enough Sleep: Sleep plays a crucial role in mood regulation. Prioritizing rest can help improve overall happiness and energy levels.

Relatable Teen Scenarios

Scenario 1: Finding Happiness in Small Moments

You wake up on a Monday morning feeling groggy. You think, *Ugh, another long school week.*

Reframing the Thought: But later, a friend cracks a joke that makes you laugh so hard you almost cry. You realize that even on tough days, small moments of joy are everywhere if you look for them.

Scenario 2: Social Media Comparison

You're scrolling through social media and see someone posting about their "perfect life", vacations, expensive clothes, tons of friends. You feel a pang of jealousy and think, *Why isn't my life like that?*

Reframing the Thought: But then you remind yourself: social media only shows highlight reels, not real life. Instead of comparing, you focus on what makes you happy, listening to your favorite music, playing a sport, or hanging out with friends.

Scenario 3: Struggling to Feel Happy

Lately, you've felt down but can't pinpoint why. You try scrolling through funny videos, but the happiness doesn't last.

Reframing the Thought: Then, you decide to go outside for a walk, listen to your favorite playlist, and call a friend. Slowly, your mood starts to shift. You realize that happiness doesn't just happen, it's something you can actively create by doing things that bring you joy.

Scenario 4: Pressure to Be Perfect

You just aced a big test, but instead of feeling happy, you immediately start stressing about the next one. You think, *If I don't keep this up, I'll fail.*

Reframing the Thought: But then, you take a moment to celebrate your success. You tell yourself, *I worked hard, and I deserve to feel proud!* You realize that happiness isn't just about achievements, it's about appreciating your progress.

"**Happiness** is not something ready-made. It comes from your own actions." — Dalai Lama

Personal Story: The Day I Stopped Chasing Happiness

For the longest time, I thought happiness was something you achieved, like unlocking a secret level in a video game. I believed it came from big, flashy milestones, writing a best-selling book, launching a successful business, or finally figuring out how to keep a plant alive (spoiler: still working on that last one). But what I didn't realize was that happiness isn't something you reach, it's something you build, moment by moment.

I remember a time when I was juggling a million things at once, businesses, writing, parenting, life. From the outside, it looked like I had everything together. But inside? I was exhausted. I told myself, *I'll feel better once I finish this book. I'll relax once this project is done. I'll be happy when…* The problem? *There was always something next on the list.*

One afternoon, I had a to-do list so long it looked like a CVS receipt. I was rushing from one thing to the next, barely taking a breath, when my son tugged on my sleeve. "Mom, can we play?" My first instinct was to say, Not right now, buddy, I'm busy. But then I looked at him, really looked at him, and saw the excitement in his eyes. I saw the moment that wouldn't wait for me.

So I did something shocking, I put my phone down. I stepped away from my work. And we played. We built LEGO towers that made no structural sense, raced cars across the floor, and laughed until our stomachs hurt. And in that moment, I realized something that changed my entire perspective:

Happiness isn't a future goal, it's happening right now.

That afternoon, there were no big achievements, no awards, no major milestones. Just laughter, connection, and the simple joy of being present. And it was one of the happiest moments of my life.

Ninja Wisdom

Happiness isn't something you chase, it's something you create with small choices every day.

Case Study: The Happiness Experiment

Maya always felt like she was missing something, even when everything seemed fine. Scrolling through social media made her feel like everyone else had a better life. One day, her friend Jordan challenged her to write down three good things each night. At first, it felt silly, but over time, she noticed small joys, laughing with friends, her favorite song on the radio, a sunny day. After a few weeks, she felt lighter, realizing happiness wasn't about having more but noticing what was already there.

Quick Quiz Box

> **Which of the following is the best way to increase happiness?**
>
> - a) Practicing gratitude every day
> - b) Waiting for good things to happen
> - c) Comparing yourself to others
> - d) Ignoring your feelings

(Answer: a) Practicing gratitude every day)

Journal Reflection Box

Write about a time when you felt genuinely happy. What were you doing? Who were you with? What made that moment special? Now, brainstorm ways to recreate that feeling in your daily life.

Action Challenge Chart

Happiness-Boosting Activity	How It Makes Me Feel	How Often I Can Do It
Practicing gratitude	Positive and grateful	Every day
Spending time with friends	Connected and happy	3-4 times a week
Exercising or moving my body	Energized and relaxed	Refocus with positive self-talk
Doing something creative	Inspired and fulfilled	Whenever I can
Helping someone else	Proud and kind	Weekly

By incorporating happiness-boosting activities into your routine, you can take control of your well-being and create more joy in your daily life. Now, let's reflect on the key takeaways from this chapter.

Chapter 5 Key Takeaways

- Happiness isn't something that happens to you, it's something you can create daily.
- Gratitude boosts serotonin, making happiness more sustainable.
- Strong social connections, movement, and mindset shifts fuel long-term joy.

Mini-FAQ

Q1: What if I don't feel happy no matter what I do?
A: Some days are tough. Focus on small wins and things that bring you comfort, happiness builds over time.

Q2: Does being happy mean ignoring my problems?
A: No! Happiness is about resilience, not pretending everything is perfect. You can work through challenges while finding joy in the process.

Happiness is important, but so is knowing how to handle sadness when it comes. In the next chapter, we'll dive into understanding and overcoming sadness in a healthy way.

6

UNDERSTANDING AND PROCESSING SADNESS

Sadness gets a bad rap. It's the emotion nobody wants to feel, the one we try to outrun, ignore, or cover up with distractions (hello, binge-watching an entire season of a show in one night). But here's the thing: Sadness isn't the villain. It's actually one of the most important emotions we have.

Sadness is what makes us human. It's a signal that something matters to us, whether it's the loss of something important, feeling left out, facing disappointment, or just having one of those days where everything feels a little off. It's normal. It's part of life. And it's not something to be ashamed of.

But here's the tricky part: staying stuck in sadness for too long can feel like sinking in quicksand. It makes it harder to see the good in yourself, in others, or in the world around you. It can lead to feeling isolated, disconnected, and convinced that things will never get better (even when they will).

That's why understanding sadness matters so much. Instead of stuffing it down or pretending it doesn't exist, we need to learn how to move through it.

What Science Says About Sadness

Dr. Brené Brown, a leading expert on emotions, explains that when we ignore sadness, it doesn't go away, it just builds up. And eventually, that emotional dam bursts. She encourages us to embrace sadness rather than suppress it, because facing our emotions is what actually helps us heal.

Neuroscientists back this up. When we process sadness in a healthy way, our brain actually rewires itself to become more resilient. That means every time you allow yourself to feel and move through sadness instead of avoiding it, you're training your brain to handle tough emotions better in the future. (Yep, emotions are basically like a mental workout.)

Riding the Waves of Sadness

Imagine sadness like ocean waves. Some are small ripples that come and go quickly, like feeling down after watching a sad movie. Others are big, crashing waves that knock you off your feet, like losing something or someone important.

Here's the key: If you fight the waves, they feel stronger. But if you let yourself ride them, they eventually pass. The goal isn't to get rid of sadness entirely (because that's impossible), but to learn how to move through it without letting it pull you under.

So the next time sadness shows up, instead of resisting it or trying to push it away, try asking yourself:

> *What is this feeling trying to tell me?*
> *Am I being kind to myself right now?*
> *Who can I talk to about this?*

Because here's the truth: Sadness doesn't last forever. And more importantly, you don't have to go through it alone.

What Sadness Feels Like in the Body

Sadness isn't just an emotion, it affects the body too:

- Low energy or feeling tired all the time
- Tightness in the chest or lump in the throat
- Loss of appetite or eating more than usual
- Trouble sleeping or wanting to sleep too much
- Difficulty focusing or staying motivated

Expert Advice

Dr. Lisa Damour, a psychologist specializing in teens, explains that sadness is often temporary. She suggests thinking of sadness like waves, sometimes strong, but always passing.

Actionable Strategies

An Emotions Ninja follows the **S.A.D.** Strategy to process sadness in a healthy way:

S – Share Your Feelings – Talk to someone you trust about what's making you sad. Keeping it inside only makes it heavier.

A – Allow Yourself to Feel – It's okay to cry or take time to process your emotions. Sadness isn't something to rush through.

D – Do Something That Brings You Comfort – Whether it's listening to music, drawing, or going for a walk, small actions can help lighten the weight of sadness.

Other techniques include:

- Writing It Out – Journaling helps organize thoughts and release emotions.
- Focusing on What You Can Control – Instead of replaying what went wrong, shift your focus to what's next.
- Connecting with Others – Even if you don't feel like socializing, spending time with people who care about you can help lift your mood.

By practicing these steps, you'll learn that sadness is something you can move through, not something that defines you.

Relatable Scenarios

Scenario 1: Losing a Friendship

You and your best friend used to talk every day, but lately, they've been hanging out with a new group and responding less to your texts. You start feeling left out, hurt, and unimportant. *Did I do something wrong? Don't I matter anymore?* The sadness sits in your chest, making it hard to focus on anything else.

Reframing the Thought: Instead of assuming the worst, you remind yourself: *Friendships change, and that doesn't mean I'm not valued. I can focus on other friendships and also reach out to my friend to check in.* You take time to process your emotions and remind yourself that you deserve friendships that make you feel included and valued.

Scenario 2: Not Getting the Outcome You Hoped For

You tried out for the basketball team, the school play, or a club position, and you really thought you had a chance. You gave it your all, but when the list goes up, your name isn't on it. The disappointment hits like a wave, and you feel not good enough.

Reframing the Thought: Instead of seeing this as a failure, you remind yourself: *This doesn't define my worth. I can use this as motivation to improve and try again next time.* You let yourself feel sad for a moment, but then you channel that energy into growing and looking for other opportunities.

Scenario 3: Feeling Alone

Lately, you feel disconnected from friends and family. Maybe you don't feel comfortable sharing your struggles, or maybe you're just feeling emotionally drained. You start thinking, *No one really understands me. Maybe I should just keep to myself.*

Reframing the Thought: Instead of withdrawing, you remind yourself: *I don't have to go through this alone.* You reach out to someone you trust, whether it's a friend, sibling, or even a teacher. You also take small steps to reconnect, joining a club, sending a text to a friend, or even just spending time around people, knowing that your feelings are temporary and you are not alone.

Scenario 4: A Tough Day That Feels Like Too Much

Some days, everything feels heavy. You spill your coffee, forget your homework, argue with a friend, and just feel off. The sadness builds up, and it feels like nothing is going right.

Reframing the Thought: Instead of letting the whole day feel ruined, you remind yourself: *One bad moment doesn't make a bad day. I can reset at any time.* You do something small that makes you feel better, listening to music, taking a deep breath, or journaling your thoughts. You remind yourself that feelings come and go, and tomorrow is a fresh start.

"**It's** okay to not be okay, as long as you are not giving up." — Karen Salmansohn

Personal Story: The Day I Stopped Fighting Sadness

For a long time, I thought sadness was something to avoid at all costs. Like stepping in a puddle with socks on, uncomfortable, annoying, and best ignored. If I felt sad, I'd push it down, plaster on a smile, and keep going. The idea of letting people see me struggle? Nope. Not happening.

But then, life threw me a curveball, not one big thing, but a bunch of small disappointments that stacked up like a teetering Jenga tower. A close friend started drifting away. I got some rough feedback on a project I had poured my heart into. At home, everything just felt a little off, tense, stressful, overwhelming. None of it was world-ending, but together? It was heavy.

At first, I did what I always did, I ignored it. I buried myself in work, filled my schedule to the brim, and distracted myself with anything that kept me too busy to *feel*. But the sadness didn't just disappear. It lingered, like an unopened text message I was too nervous to read.

One morning, my teacher, who, let's be real, has supernatural teacher senses, noticed I wasn't quite myself. She sat next to me and simply asked, "How are you feeling?" My instinct was to brush it off with the classic *I'm fine*. But something in me cracked, and before I knew it, I admitted, *I just feel sad, and I don't even know why.*

Instead of rushing in with advice or trying to "fix" it, she just nodded and said something I'll never forget: "It's okay to feel sad. You don't have to have a reason. Just let yourself feel it."

That moment changed everything. I stopped fighting sadness like it was the enemy. Instead, I started giving it space, writing in my journal, going for walks, and actually talking to people instead of pretending everything was fine. And slowly? The sadness became lighter. Manageable. Less overwhelming.

Lesson learned: Feeling sad doesn't mean you're weak, it means you're human. And like any other emotion, sadness passes when you stop trying to outrun it and just let yourself feel.

Ninja Wisdom

Sadness isn't a sign of weakness, it's proof that you care deeply. Let yourself feel it, then take small steps forward.

Case Study: The Friendship Shift

Elliot's best friend started hanging out with a new group, and he felt forgotten. Instead of bottling it up, he wrote his feelings in a journal and talked to his friend. They worked it out, and he learned that sadness wasn't a weakness, it was a sign that something mattered to him.

Quick Quiz Box

What's the best way to handle sadness?

- a) Talk to someone and take care of yourself
- b) Pretend you're fine and ignore it
- c) Keep everything bottled up
- d) Avoid anything that reminds you of your sadness

(Answer: a) *Talk to someone and take care of yourself*)

Journal Reflection Box

Write about a time when you felt sad. What helped you move forward?

Action Challenge Chart

Sadness Trigger	My Initial Reaction	A Healthier Response
Losing a friendship	Withdrawing completely	Talking about it with someone I trust
Disappointing news	Feeling stuck	Writing my feelings in a journal
A tough day	Avoiding everyone	Doing something that brings me comfort

Try these strategies next time you feel sad.

Chapter 6 Key Takeaways

- Sadness is a normal emotion, not something to fear.
- Allowing yourself to feel sadness helps you move through it.
- Talking to someone or doing comforting activities can lighten the weight.

Mini-FAQ

Q1: What if I don't want to talk about my sadness?
A: That's okay. Try writing your feelings down or engaging in calming activities. Sharing helps, but processing in your own way is valid too.

Q2: How long does sadness last?
A: It depends, but giving yourself space to feel and heal helps it pass more easily.

Sadness teaches us to slow down and reflect. Now, let's talk about patience, why it's a superpower and how practicing delayed gratification can lead to success.

7

THE POWER OF PATIENCE

Patience isn't just about waiting in long lines at the coffee shop without losing your mind, it's about mastering the art of self-control. It's about choosing long-term rewards over instant gratification (even when instant gratification is a double chocolate chip cookie staring you in the face). In a world where everything is available at lightning speed, waiting for anything feels *painful*. But here's the secret: patience isn't just about waiting, it's about making smarter choices that set you up for success.

Think about it: The ability to pause and think before acting can lead to better financial stability, improved health, stronger relationships, and long-term happiness. Want to build wealth? Patience helps you save money instead of impulse-buying things you'll regret later (hello, late-night online shopping). Want to be healthier? Patience helps you stick to habits that actually make a difference instead of chasing quick fixes. Want deeper friendships and relationships? Patience teaches you to listen, to wait, and to grow alongside others instead of demanding immediate results.

But let's be real, waiting is hard. Whether it's refreshing your phone for a text reply, standing in a never-ending line, or counting down the days to an exciting event, patience feels like a muscle that constantly needs stretching. Without it, frustration takes over, leading to impulsive decisions, unnecessary stress, and the regret of eating an entire bag of chips because you "just couldn't wait" for dinner.

The Science of Patience

Dr. Dan Ariely, a behavioral economist, explains that patience is like a mental muscle, the more you practice small acts of self-control, the stronger it gets. He suggests starting small:

- Wait five extra minutes before checking social media. Your notifications aren't going anywhere, and delaying the scroll session helps train your brain to resist the urge for instant dopamine hits.
- Save small amounts of money instead of impulse spending. Instead of buying that random gadget you'll forget about in two weeks, practice delaying gratification and putting that money toward something meaningful.
- Pause before reacting. Whether it's a frustrating email, an annoying sibling, or a slow driver in front of you, take a deep breath before you react. One moment of patience can save a whole lot of unnecessary stress.

So the next time you're tempted to rush into something, remind yourself: Patience isn't about waiting, it's about choosing what's worth waiting for.

What Impatience Feels Like in the Body

When someone is impatient, they may feel jittery, their legs bouncing up and down, or their fingers tapping anxiously. There's often a tightness in the chest, an overwhelming urge to act immediately, and frustration bubbling just beneath the surface. The mind races, making it hard to focus on anything but what they want right now.

How Delayed Gratification Leads to Success

1. Financial Wealth: People who practice delayed gratification make smarter money decisions. Instead of spending impulsively, they save and invest for the future, leading to financial freedom and security. For example, instead of buying the latest phone, a patient person might invest that money in a savings account or stocks, watching their wealth grow over time.
2. Good Health: Healthy habits require patience. Choosing a nutritious meal over fast food or exercising instead of watching TV may not bring instant pleasure, but in the long run, these decisions result in a healthier body, more energy, and a longer life.
3. Stronger Friendships and Relationships: In social settings, patience leads to better communication, trust, and understanding. Whether in friendships, dating, or marriage, being able to listen, compromise, and resolve conflicts calmly makes relationships last. Instead of reacting emotionally in an argument, taking time to process emotions leads to healthier interactions.

Expert Advice

Dr. Walter Mischel, the psychologist behind the famous Marshmallow Test, found that children who were able to delay gratification, waiting for a larger reward rather than taking an immediate, smaller one, grew up to have better academic success, healthier relationships, and improved self-control.

Actionable Strategies

An Emotions Ninja practices the **Three Ts** to build patience:

- **Think** through the consequences before making impulsive decisions.
- **Tell** yourself: Good things come to those who wait.

- **Take** deep breaths when feeling impatient.

Other patience-building strategies include:

- Using distractions like listening to music or engaging in another task while waiting.
- Practicing mindfulness to stay present instead of obsessing over future outcomes.
- Setting long-term goals to train delayed gratification.

Try using these strategies and note how they develop your delayed gratification!

Relatable Teen Scenarios

Scenario 1: Studying for a Big Exam

Your final exam is coming up, and you have two choices: cram the night before and hope for the best, or study a little each day and be fully prepared.

Making the Wise Choice: You choose to space out your studying, even though it's tempting to scroll through your phone instead. On test day, you feel confident and relaxed, knowing that your patience and effort have paid off.

Scenario 2: Saving Money for Something You Really Want

You've been wanting the newest sneakers for months, but they're expensive.

Making the Wise Choice: Instead of spending your money on small things like snacks and games, you decide to save up little by little. Every time you add to your savings, you remind yourself: *This is worth it.* After a few months, you finally buy the sneakers with your own money, and the feeling is so much better than if you had taken a shortcut.

Scenario 3: Waiting for a Text Back

You send an important text to a friend, and minutes feel like hours as you wait for a reply. You start overthinking: *Are they mad at me? Did I say something wrong?*

Making the Wise Choice: Instead of spiraling into frustration, you distract yourself with something fun, playing a game, reading, or going outside. When your friend finally responds, you realize they were just busy and there was no need to stress.

Scenario 4: Getting Better at a Sport or Skill

You've been practicing your free throws in basketball, but you still miss more than you make. You start thinking, *Maybe I'm just not good at this.*

Making the Wise Choice: But instead of quitting, you keep practicing every day. A few weeks later, you step onto the court and sink shot after shot, your patience and effort finally pay off.

"**Patience** is not the ability to wait, but the ability to keep a good attitude while waiting." — Joyce Meyer

Personal Story: The Slow Road to Success

When I was younger, patience was not my thing. I wanted everything, and I wanted it fast, success, results, and, let's be real, dessert before dinner. If something took too long, I'd immediately get frustrated. But one experience changed the way I saw patience, not as pointless waiting, but as the secret ingredient to success.

Back in elementary school, reading and writing felt like trying to solve a Rubik's Cube blindfolded, other kids seemed to breeze through books while I was stuck in the mud, sounding out words at a snail's pace. *Why is this so hard for me?* I wondered. I wanted to be good right away, but no matter how hard I tried, improvement felt painfully slow.

Enter Mrs. Ruth Payne, my teacher and, looking back, my personal patience coach. She could've just let me struggle, but instead, she stayed after school with me, breaking down words one step at a time. I didn't become a reading genius overnight, no magical transformation, no movie montage where suddenly I was top of the class. But little by little, I got better.

Then, something wild happened. By second grade, I had improved so much that I skipped a grade. Me, the kid who thought I'd never catch up. That's when I realized: patience and consistent effort are the real game-changers. If I had given up early just because progress felt slow, I would've never seen what I was truly capable of.

That lesson stuck with me for life. Whether it's in business, writing, or just navigating the wild ride of life itself, I know now that real success isn't about speed, it's about showing up, sticking with it, and trusting the process. Because the best things? They take time.

Ninja Wisdom

Patience isn't about waiting, it's about making smart choices that lead to long-term success. Patience isn't about waiting, it's about how you act while waiting.

Case Study: The Instant Gratification Experiment

Alex wanted the newest gaming console but didn't have enough money. Instead of begging his parents, he saved up for months. When he finally bought it himself, he felt a deep sense of accomplishment, way better than if he'd gotten it instantly.

Quick Quiz Box

When you're waiting in a long line, what is the best way to handle impatience?

- a) Complain about how slow it is
- b) Take deep breaths and distract yourself
- c) Try to cut ahead
- d) Give up and leave

(Answer: b) Take deep breaths and distract yourself)

Journal Reflection Box

Think of a time when you had to wait for something you really wanted. How did you feel? What did you do to pass the time? Looking back, do you think waiting made the outcome more rewarding?

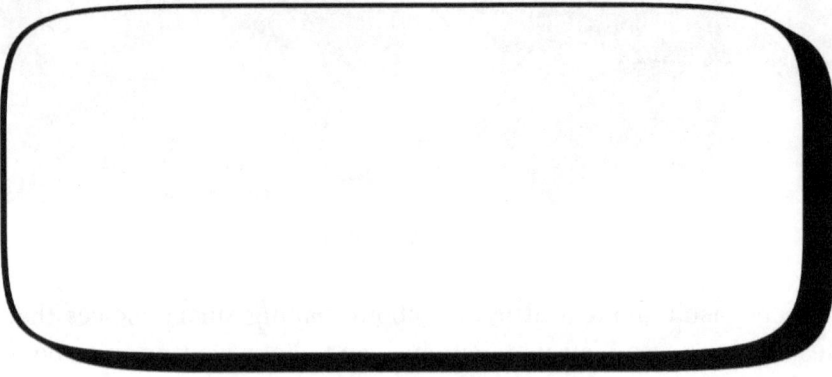

Action Challenge Chart

Situation	Initial Reaction	Alternative Response Using the Three Ts
Waiting for test results	Checking email obsessively	Taking deep breaths and focusing on other tasks
Saving money for something big	Spending on small things	Tell or remind yourself of the end goal and resisting impulse buys
Urge to do something impulsive	Rushing a decision	Think through the consequences

Try these strategies next time you're feeling impatient.

Chapter 7 Key Takeaways

- Patience isn't about waiting, it's about handling the wait well.
- Delayed gratification leads to better decision-making and long-term success.
- Taking deep breaths and thinking before reacting builds self-control.

Mini-FAQ

Q1: How can I be patient when I want results now?
A: Break it down. Focus on small steps and celebrate progress instead of just the final result.

Q2: What if patience makes me feel like I'm falling behind?
A: Patience isn't about doing nothing, it's about smart persistence. Keep moving forward, even if progress feels slow.

Patience helps us handle life's challenges, but what about the worries that creep in? In the next chapter, we'll learn how to manage worry and keep it from taking over our thoughts.

THE POWER OF PATIENCE

8

OVERCOMING WORRY AND FINDING PEACE

Picture this: your mind is throwing a non-stop party for every single worry you've ever had, complete with confetti cannons and neon strobe lights. Exciting, right? Except instead of fun, it's all the little "What if…" questions swirling around, shouting over each other and generally making you feel like you need a vacation from your own brain. That's worry for you.

But guess what? You're not alone, and you're definitely not doomed. Everyone has that occasional mental circus where stress clowns and anxiety elephants parade around. It's part of being human, especially a teen. You've got friendships to manage, teachers to impress, snap judgments (and Snapchats) to handle, and a whole future to figure out. It's kind of a big deal! So of course some nerves are going to pop up here and there.

The great news is that those worries can be tamed. In fact, a bit of worry can even be helpful (yep, you read that right). It can keep you on your toes, reminding you to study for tests or double-check your homework. The trick is making sure those little nagging concerns don't overtake your life like the latest viral dance challenge. By learning to understand what triggers your worries, focusing only on what you can control and giving yourself some tools to manage worry, you can rock that unstoppable, feel-good confidence, no clown wig required.

What Worry Feels Like in the Body

Worry isn't just something that happens in your head, it shows up everywhere. It's like your brain hits the panic button, even when there's no actual emergency. Suddenly, your body is on high alert, preparing for a disaster that isn't coming. The worst part? Your body doesn't know the difference between real danger and imaginary stress, so it reacts the same way.

Physical Symptoms of Worry

- Tension headaches & jaw clenching – Because apparently, your stress loves to hang out in your face.
- Rapid heartbeat & shortness of breath – Like you just ran a marathon… without moving an inch.
- Tightness in the chest or stomach aches – That "pit in your stomach" feeling? Yep, that's worry, making itself at home.
- Restlessness or difficulty falling asleep – Because what better time to replay embarrassing moments from five years ago than at 2 AM?
- Fatigue & muscle tension – Your body has been on "fight-or-flight" mode all day, and now it's just exhausted.

Emotional Effects of Worry

1. Overthinking & worst-case-scenario spirals – One small concern turns into an elaborate disaster movie playing in your head.
2. Irritability & mood swings – Worry doesn't just mess with you, it makes everyone around you wonder if you woke up on the wrong side of the bed.

3. Difficulty concentrating or making decisions – Should you text first? Should you eat pasta or a sandwich? Even simple choices feel impossible.
4. Sense of dread or feeling overwhelmed – Like an imaginary storm cloud following you everywhere.
5. Avoiding situations out of fear – If you just don't deal with it, maybe it will magically go away (spoiler: it won't).

The Bottom Line

Worry can be useful, it helps us prepare for challenges and make thoughtful choices. But too much worry? That's when things go sideways. When worry takes over, your body reacts with stress signals that keep you in a constant state of tension. The key is learning how to turn down the volume on worry so it doesn't run the show.

The good news? You're about to learn how to stop worry in its tracks, before it takes over.

Expert Advice

Dr. Judson Brewer, a neuroscientist specializing in anxiety, explains that worry is often a habit our brain forms. He suggests breaking the worry loop by replacing anxious thoughts with curiosity, ask yourself, *What else could happen that is positive?*

Actionable Strategies

An Emotions Ninja learns to let go of what they can't control and focus on what they can.

The Circle of Control – One of the most powerful tools for managing worry is understanding what is within and outside your control.

How to Use It: Draw a large circle on a piece of paper. Inside the circle, write things you can control. Outside the circle, write things you cannot control. Whenever you start worrying, check your Circle of Control, if it's inside, take action; if it's outside, let it go.

What's Inside a Teen's Circle of Control?

- Your attitude and mindset
- How much effort you put into studying or sports
- How you respond to challenges
- The words you choose to say
- Your daily habits (exercise, sleep, nutrition)
- How you treat friends and family
- Asking for help when needed

What's Outside a Teen's Circle of Control?

- Other people's opinions or reactions
- The outcome of a test after you've studied
- What others say about you on social media
- Unexpected events (weather, school cancellations, illness)
- Other people's emotions or actions
- The past, things that have already happened

By focusing on what's inside your Circle of Control, you take back your power and stop wasting energy on things you can't change. Instead of feeling helpless, you can take action and feel more in control of your life.. Outside the circle, write what you CAN'T control, like what others think or do. Instead of stressing over what's outside your control, focus on taking action within your circle.

Blowing the Dandelion – When worry starts to spiral, imagine holding a dandelion. As you take a deep breath in, visualize all your worries in the fluffy white seeds. Then, exhale slowly, imagining the seeds floating away, carrying your worries with them. This method helps calm the mind and release anxious thoughts.

Other techniques include:

- Reframing Thoughts – Replace *What if everything goes wrong?* with *What if things actually go right?*

- Journaling Your Worries – Writing your worries down helps clear your mind and organize thoughts.
- Progressive Muscle Relaxation – Tense and relax different muscle groups to release tension.
- Setting a "Worry Time" – Give yourself 10 minutes a day to think about worries, then move on with your day.

Try these techniques and notice how managing worry helps you feel calmer and more in control!

Real-Life Scenarios

Scenario 1: Worrying About a Big Test

You have a huge test coming up, and you can't stop thinking about it. Your mind keeps repeating: *What if I fail? What if I forget everything I studied? What if I let my parents down?* Your stomach tightens, your heart races, and you feel stuck in a cycle of overthinking.

Reframing the Thought: Instead of worrying about what *could* go wrong, you remind yourself: *I've studied, and I'm prepared. Even if I don't get a perfect score, one test won't define me.* You take deep breaths, review your notes one last time, and remind yourself that worrying won't change the outcome, but preparation will.

Scenario 2: Overthinking a Social Situation

You had a conversation with a friend, and later, you start replaying every word you said in your head. *Did I sound weird? What if they took it the wrong way? What if they don't want to be my friend anymore?* The more you think about it, the more your anxiety grows.

Reframing the Thought: Instead of assuming the worst, you remind yourself: *I don't have to read into every small detail, my friend wouldn't stop talking to me over one conversation.* You distract yourself with a book, a game, or music to get out of your own head, realizing that most of the time, people aren't overanalyzing you as much as you think.

Scenario 3: Worrying About the Future

You start thinking about college, careers, and your future. The questions pile up in your mind: *What if I pick the wrong major? What if I don't get into a good school? What if I fail in life?* Suddenly, the future feels too big and overwhelming.

     Reframing the Thought: Instead of panicking over everything at once, you remind yourself: *I don't have to have my whole life figured out right now.* You focus on one step at a time, choosing classes you enjoy, exploring your interests, and trusting that the future will unfold one decision at a time.

Scenario 4: Stressing Over What You Can't Control

Your friend is in a bad mood, and they're acting distant. You start thinking: *Did I do something wrong? Are they mad at me?* You start worrying nonstop, even though you have no proof that it's about you.

     Reframing the Thought: Instead of assuming the worst, you remind yourself: *Their mood isn't my responsibility. If something is wrong, they'll tell me.* You focus on what you can control, sending a kind message to check in and then letting go of what you can't control.

"**Worrying** is like a rocking chair. It gives you something to do but gets you nowhere."
— Erma Bombeck

Personal Story

When I was younger, worry felt like my shadow, always following me around, whispering worst-case scenarios into my mind. I worried about school, friendships, the future, everything. But there was one experience that truly showed me how worry can take over if you let it, and how learning to manage it can change everything.

I remember one year when my family was going through a difficult time financially. Even though my parents tried to shield me from stress, I could feel the tension in the air. I started worrying about things I had never thought about before: *What if we lose our house? What if my parents can't afford groceries? What if things never get better?*

At night, I would lie in bed, my mind racing with 'what ifs'. My stomach would tighten, my chest felt heavy, and no matter how much I tried to distract myself, I couldn't shake the constant anxiety. I felt like I had to solve everything, even though I was just a kid.

One evening, I overheard my mom talking to my dad. She was calm and steady, even though I knew things weren't easy. She said something that changed the way I saw worry forever:

"Worrying won't change what happens tomorrow, but it will steal your peace today."

That sentence stuck with me. I realized that I had been spending so much energy stressing over things I couldn't control, instead of focusing on the things I *could* do.

From that moment on, I started training my brain to handle worry differently. Instead of letting my thoughts spiral, I would ask myself: *Is this something I can control?* If the answer was yes, I would take action, like studying harder for a test instead of just worrying about failing. If the answer was no, I would remind myself: *I've done my best, and worrying won't change the outcome.*

Now, whenever I feel worry creeping in, I picture myself blowing on a dandelion, watching each little seed float away. It

> reminds me that some things are out of my hands, and that's okay. I learned that worry doesn't have to control me, I can choose to let go, breathe, and focus on the present.

Ninja Wisdom

Worry is a visitor, not a permanent resident. You can learn to show it the door.

Case Study: The Overthinking Spiral

Ava worried about everything, tests, friendships, even weather forecasts. Her mind was like a hamster on a wheel, running through worst-case scenarios at full speed. One day, she forgot her homework at home and panicked. *What if my teacher yells at me? What if I fail?* Her friend Jake noticed and said, "Okay, let's be real. Is your teacher actually a fire-breathing dragon, or are you overthinking?" That made Ava laugh, and she realized she was catastrophizing. She practiced deep breathing and reminded herself, *One mistake won't ruin everything.* And guess what? Her teacher just told her to bring it tomorrow.

Quick Quiz Box

What's the best way to stop worrying?

- a) Focus on the present and take deep breaths
- b) Overthink the situation to prepare for every outcome
- c) Avoid the problem and hope it goes away
- d) Assume the worst and stress about it

(Answer: a) Focus on the present and take deep breaths)

Journal Reflection Box

Write about a recent time you felt worried. What was the worst-case scenario? How did it actually turn out?

Action Challenge Chart

Worry Trigger	Initial Reaction	Better Response
Big test	Panic and overthink	Focus on what I can control - study
Social anxiety	Avoid talking to people	Deep breath; pretend to blow a dandelion
Fear of failure	Assume the worst	Ask myself what's the worst that can happen

Try these strategies next time you feel worried.

Chapter 8 Key Takeaways

- Worrying doesn't solve problems, taking action does.

- Focus on what you can control and let go of the rest.
- Grounding techniques help bring your mind back to the present.

Mini-FAQ

Q1: What if I can't stop worrying?
A: Worrying is a habit, train your brain to focus on solutions rather than spiraling into what-ifs.

Q2: How do I handle things outside my control?
A: Use The Circle of Control, let go of what you can't change and focus on what you can.

Worry often focuses on what could go wrong, but a positive mindset helps us see what could go right. In the next chapter, we'll explore how shifting your perspective can change your life.

9

SHIFTING YOUR MINDSET

Your brain is like a superpowered filter, the way you choose to see the world determines what you experience. A positive mindset doesn't mean pretending everything is fine when it's not, it means looking at challenges as opportunities instead of doom-filled disasters.

Perspective Is Everything

You've probably heard the whole *glass half full vs. glass half empty* analogy. But let's put that into real life terms:

- Fail a test? You can either say, *"Welp, I'm just bad at this subject"* (half empty) OR *"Okay, what can I learn from this so I do better next time?"* (half full).
- A friend cancels plans? You can dwell on the rejection (*"They don't want to hang out with me"*) OR use the free time for self-care (*"Guess I have time to binge my favorite show and wear pajamas all day!"*).

Your Thoughts = Your Reality

When you shift your mindset, you're not ignoring problems, you're training your brain to look for solutions instead of spiraling into self-doubt. Studies show that negative thinking fuels stress, anxiety, and fear, while a resilient, problem-solving mindset leads to confidence, motivation, and growth. Basically, your thoughts have power, use them wisely.

How a Positive Mindset Helps in Life

- Academic Success: A growth mindset helps you see challenges as learning opportunities rather than failures.
- Better Relationships: Positive people attract and maintain healthy friendships by focusing on understanding rather than blame.
- Increased Confidence: Seeing setbacks as temporary helps you stay motivated and resilient.

What Negative Thinking Feels Like in the Body

When your brain goes into worst-case-scenario mode, your body feels it too. You might notice:

- Feeling weighed down, like you're carrying a backpack full of bricks
- Tension in your shoulders and neck, like you've been bench-pressing stress
- Lack of motivation, where even brushing your teeth feels like an Olympic sport
- Racing thoughts, running every worst-case scenario as if your brain is a 24/7 disaster news channel

The good news? You have the power to shift your perspective. And once you do, you'll start seeing opportunities instead of roadblocks, and life suddenly feels a whole lot lighter.

Expert Advice

Dr. Lisa Damour, a clinical psychologist specializing in adolescent development, emphasizes the power of perspective-taking. She suggests that teens who practice looking at situations from different angles develop stronger emotional regulation and problem-solving skills. She advises, '*When something feels overwhelming, take a step back and ask yourself: How else can I interpret this situation? Is there another way to look at it?*'

Actionable Strategies

An Emotions Ninja uses the **Deep Breath Reset** Method:

1. Pause and recognize your negative thoughts.
2. Inhale deeply for four seconds while imagining drawing in calm energy.
3. Hold the breath for four seconds, allowing yourself to process the thought.
4. Exhale slowly for six seconds, releasing the negativity and making room for a positive perspective.
5. Replace the thought with an empowering and hopeful perspective.*

Other mindset-shifting strategies include:

- Gratitude practice: Listing three things you're grateful for each day
- Reframing: Turning "I can't" into "I can try"
- Surrounding yourself with positive influences
- Try using these strategies and see how shifting your mindset changes your outlook!

Relatable Teen Scenarios

Scenario 1: Getting a Bad Grade on a Test

You studied hard for your math test, but when you get it back, your stomach drops, you didn't do as well as you hoped. *I'll never be good at this*, you think.

>Reframing the Thought: But instead of letting negativity take over, you tell yourself, *This is just one test. I can learn from my mistakes and do better next time.* You go over what you missed, ask for help, and study differently for the next one. A few weeks later, you improve your score, and your confidence.

Scenario 2: Feeling Left Out

You see pictures on social media of your friends hanging out without you. Your first thought is, *They don't like me anymore.* You feel hurt and left out.

>Reframing the Thought: But instead of dwelling on what you don't know, you remind yourself: *They might have made last-minute plans, and that doesn't mean they don't care about me.* You decide to reach out, make your own plans, and focus on the friends who value you. By shifting your mindset, you avoid unnecessary worry and self-doubt.

Scenario 3: Trying Something New

You've always wanted to learn how to skateboard, but after a few tries, you keep falling and getting frustrated. You think, *I'm just not good at this.*

>Reframing the Thought: But then you remember: *No one is great at something the first time they try.* Instead of giving up, you laugh it off and keep practicing. A few weeks later, you land your first trick, and the feeling is worth every fall.

Scenario 4: Dealing with Criticism

You work really hard on an art project, but when your teacher gives feedback, all you hear are the things you need to improve. You start thinking, *I'm not talented enough.*

Reframing the Thought: But instead of taking it personally, you reframe it: *This feedback will help me get even better.* You take the suggestions, practice, and turn in a revised piece that makes you proud. By choosing to see criticism as growth, you keep improving.

"A negative mind will never give you a positive life."
— Unknown

Personal Story

When I was younger, I didn't always have a positive mindset. If something went wrong, I would get frustrated, doubt myself, or assume the worst. One experience, in particular, stands out.

In middle school, I tried out for a school competition. I spent weeks preparing, practicing every day, and visualizing myself winning. But when the results were posted, my name wasn't on the list. My stomach dropped. *All that hard work for nothing, I thought. I guess I'm just not good enough.*

I felt like giving up, but then I remembered something my teacher once told me: *Every setback is a setup for something greater.* Instead of staying stuck in negativity, I decided to reframe my thoughts: *Maybe I didn't win this time, but that doesn't mean I won't succeed in the future.* I kept working on my skills, and the next year, I not only made the competition, I placed in the top three.

That experience changed my perspective. I realized that setbacks don't mean failure; they mean you're learning, growing, and getting better. A positive mindset doesn't mean ignoring challenges, it means choosing to believe that challenges will make you stronger.

Ninja Wisdom

You can't control the thoughts you have, but you can choose which ones to focus on.

Case Study: The Great Reframe

Jace failed his driving test and immediately thought, I'll never get my license. His dad, who had clearly been reading motivational posters, said, "Failure is just feedback." Jace rolled his eyes but gave it another shot. Instead of beating himself up, he looked at what he did wrong, practiced more, and took the test again.

This time? He passed. That's when he realized setbacks weren't roadblocks, they were just detours.

Quick Quiz Box

When faced with a setback, what is the best way to respond?

- a) Give up and accept failure
- b) Ignore it and move on
- c) Find a lesson in it and try again
- d) Blame others

(Answer: c) Find a lesson in it and try again)

Journal Reflection Box

Write about a time when you felt really negative about a situation. What was the outcome? Could a positive mindset have changed it?

Action Challenge Chart

Situation	Negative Thought	Positive Reframe
Messing up in a game	I'm terrible at this	I can improve with practice
Getting a low test score	I'm not smart enough	I can study differently and do better next time
Facing a challenge	This is too hard	I can figure it out step by step

Try these strategies next time you feel negative.

Chapter 9 Key Takeaways

- Your thoughts shape your reality, reframing negative thoughts changes how you feel.
- Gratitude and self-talk can help build a more optimistic mindset.
- Challenges aren't failures, they're opportunities to learn and grow.

Mini-FAQ

Q1: What if positive thinking feels fake?
A: You don't have to pretend, just start shifting one thought at a time. Even small adjustments help.

Q2: Can I be positive but still realistic?
A: Absolutely! Positivity doesn't mean ignoring problems, it means facing them with a solutions-focused mindset.

Positivity is powerful, but stress is still a part of life. The key is learning how to manage it. In the next chapter, we'll explore techniques to stay calm and handle stress like a ninja.

10

FINDING CALM IN CHAOS

Stress is like that one over dramatic friend, sometimes helpful, sometimes way too much to handle. A little bit of stress? That's the push that helps you meet deadlines, stay focused, and get things done. But too much stress? That's when things get messy, cue sleepless nights, mood swings, and feeling like your brain is a browser with 87 tabs open.

The key? Managing stress before it manages you.

The Big Picture: Why Managing Stress Now Matters for Your Future

Stress is a part of life, but how you handle it determines your success. It can either be a fuel that helps you grow or a fire that burns you out. The difference? How you respond to it.

In small amounts, stress is actually helpful. It pushes you to meet deadlines, sharpen your focus, and get things done. But when stress goes unchecked, it starts controlling you instead of motivating you. That's when it leads to overwhelm, anxiety, and exhaustion.

Here's the truth: How you handle stress today sets the foundation for how you'll handle challenges in the future. Whether it's college exams, job pressures, relationships, or unexpected life events, stress never disappears, but your ability to manage it can make all the difference.

Think about successful athletes, musicians, and leaders. Do they never experience stress? Of course not! The difference is, they've trained themselves to handle pressure without falling apart. Learning to manage stress now will set you up for a life where you can handle challenges with resilience instead of panic.

The Science of Stress (a.k.a. Why Your Body Freaks Out)

Dr. Stephen Porges, a neuroscientist known for his work on the Polyvagal Theory, explains that grounding techniques(like deep breathing, humming, or engaging your senses) can activate the vagus nerve, which is basically your body's "chill out" switch. When stress is handled properly, it can motivate you to push through challenges and build resilience instead of feeling like you're stuck in a never-ending fight-or-flight mode.

What Stress Feels Like in the Body

Stress triggers your body's emergency alarm system, a.k.a. the fight-or-flight response, which was originally designed to protect you from saber-toothed tigers. The problem? Your brain reacts the same way to an overdue assignment as it would to an actual life-threatening danger.

Here's what stress does to your body:

- Heart Rate & Breathing Go Haywire – Your body sends oxygen to your muscles like you're about to sprint… even if you're just sitting in math class.
- Muscle Tension – Your shoulders, neck, and jaw feel tight, like you've been bench-pressing your problems all day.

- Digestive Issues – Ever felt nauseous before a big test? That's because stress can throw your stomach into full chaos mode, leading to bloating, nausea, or even IBS (Irritable Bowel Syndrome).
- Fatigue & Trouble Sleeping – Your brain is like, "*We should stay awake and replay embarrassing moments from five years ago!*", which makes relaxing nearly impossible. Weakened Immune System – Too much stress = more colds, more exhaustion, and more feeling like a half-charged phone.

The Bottom Line?

Stress isn't the enemy, it's how you handle it that makes the difference. Learning how to flip the switch from stress mode to chill mode is a superpower that will help you focus, sleep better, and actually enjoy life instead of constantly bracing for impact. And the best part? You're about to learn exactly how to do it.

Expert Advice

Dr. Judson Brewer, a psychiatrist specializing in anxiety management, recommends mindfulness-based grounding exercises. He states that focusing on sensation-based experiences, like touching a cold surface or listening to environmental sounds, helps the brain detach from worry cycles and find calm.

Actionable Strategies

An Emotions Ninja uses the **5-4-3-2-1 Grounding Method**:

- Find **5** things you can see
- Find **4** things you can touch
- Find **3** things you can hear
- Find **2** things you can smell
- Find **1** thing you can taste

What Is Grounding?

Grounding is a set of techniques used to bring focus back to the present moment and reduce overwhelming emotions. When stress takes over, grounding helps anchor you in reality, shifting attention away from anxious thoughts and back to your body and surroundings.

How Grounding Helps the Body

- Activates the parasympathetic nervous system, which counteracts the fight-or-flight response and promotes relaxation.
- Lowers cortisol levels, reducing the long-term negative effects of stress.
- Improves focus and decision-making, allowing for clearer thinking in high-pressure situations.
- Helps regulate breathing and heart rate, restoring a sense of calm.

There are different types of grounding:

1. Barefoot Grounding (Earthing) – Walking barefoot on grass, soil, or sand can regulate the body's electrical charge and lower stress.
2. Breath Control (Physiological Sigh) – Two short inhales through the nose, followed by a long exhale through the mouth helps quickly reset the nervous system and bring immediate relief.
3. Temperature Shifts – Holding an ice cube, splashing cold water on your face, or taking a cold shower can instantly shift focus away from stress and into the body.
4. Body Awareness (Progressive Muscle Relaxation) – Tensing and then slowly relaxing muscle groups one by one helps release physical tension stored in the body.

Other stress management strategies include:

- Prioritization: Write down everything you need to do and tackle one thing at a time.
- Deep breathing exercises: Inhale for 4 seconds, hold for 4 seconds, exhale for 6 seconds.
- Physical movement: Exercise, stretch, or take a walk to release tension.
- Try these grounding strategies and observe how they shift your response to stress!

Relatable Teen Scenarios

Scenario 1: Feeling Overwhelmed with Schoolwork

You have three tests, a paper due, and a group project all in the same week. The more you think about it, the more overwhelmed and stressed you feel. Your brain starts repeating, *I'll never get all this done!* Your first instinct is to procrastinate because it all feels too much.

Reframing the Thought: Instead of letting stress take over, you break things down into smaller steps. You make a to-do list, start with one task, and take breaks in between. By the end of the week, you realize that tackling things one step at a time makes them manageable, and that you had more control than you thought.

Scenario 2: Balancing Extracurriculars and Social Life

You love playing soccer, being in student council, and hanging out with friends, but lately, it feels like there's not enough time for everything. You're exhausted, stretched too thin, and worrying about disappointing people.

Reframing the Thought: Instead of trying to do everything, you take a step back and prioritize what matters most. You talk to your coach about adjusting your schedule and set boundaries for when you need time for yourself. You realize that saying no sometimes is necessary to protect your well-being.

Scenario 3: Preparing for a Big Presentation

Public speaking makes your heart race and palms sweat. Your presentation is tomorrow, and every time you think about it, you get more anxious. You start picturing *everything that could go wrong*, forgetting your words, tripping in front of the class, people laughing.

Reframing the Thought: Instead of focusing on what could go wrong, you practice what could go right. You rehearse in front of a mirror, take deep breaths, and remind yourself, *I've prepared for this. I don't have to be perfect, I just have to try my best.* When it's time to present, you're still nervous, but you push through, and it goes better than expected.

Scenario 4: Handling Conflict with a Friend

Your best friend suddenly starts acting distant. They're not responding to texts, and when you see them at school, they barely talk to you. Your brain immediately jumps to, *Did I do something wrong? Are they mad at me?* You feel stressed and upset, replaying past conversations trying to figure it out.

Reframing the Thought: Instead of assuming the worst, you decide to communicate. You send a simple text: *Hey, I've noticed you've been quiet lately. Is everything okay?* Your friend replies that they've been going through a tough time with their family and needed space. You realize that sometimes, stress isn't about you, it's about what others are dealing with, too.

"It's not stress that kills us, it is our reaction to it."
— Hans Selye

> **Personal Story**
>
> When I was younger, I put a lot of pressure on myself to be perfect, especially in school. I wanted to get the best grades, be involved in everything, and make my parents proud. But one year, I hit a breaking point.
>
> I had a huge test coming up, a project due, and extracurricular commitments all at the same time. No matter how much I studied, I felt like I wasn't doing enough. My thoughts raced: *What if I fail? What if I let everyone down?* The stress built up so much that I started losing sleep, feeling exhausted, and struggling to focus.
>
> One day, my teacher pulled me aside and said, *You don't have to do everything at once. Take a step back and focus on what you can control.* That advice changed everything for me. I started breaking tasks into smaller steps, taking study breaks, and letting go of the need to be perfect. I learned that stress doesn't mean I'm failing, it means I need to pause, breathe, and reset.
>
> From that moment on, I realized that managing stress isn't about doing more, it's about taking care of yourself so you can do your best.

Ninja Wisdom

Stress happens, but you have the power to stay calm and in control.

Case Study: The Homework Avalanche

Sophia had three tests, a group project, and an essay due in the same week. This is it, she thought. This is how I die, from academic exhaustion. Instead of panicking, she used the "break it down" method, tackling one task at a time, setting timers for focus, and rewarding herself with dance breaks. By the end of the week, she survived, realized stress was manageable, and did not die from excessive schoolwork.

Quick Quiz Box

Which of the following is a grounding technique?

- a) Focusing on deep breathing and engaging the senses
- b) Ignoring stress and hoping it goes away
- c) Letting anxious thoughts spiral
- d) Watching TV as a distraction

(Answer: a) Focusing on deep breathing and engaging the senses)

Journal Reflection Box

Think of a time when stress felt overwhelming. What grounding techniques have you tried? How did they help? What will you try next time?

Action Challenge Chart

Stressful Situation	How My Body Reacted	Grounding Technique to Try
Feeling overwhelmed with schoolwork	Racing heart, tight chest	5-4-3-2-1 grounding method
Public speaking anxiety	Sweaty palms, shaky hands	Deep breathing with a physiological sigh
Conflict with a friend	Stomach pain, tense muscles	Progressive muscle relaxation

Manage stress levels by using one of the strategies next time!

Chapter 10 Key Takeaways

- Stress is a normal reaction, but how you handle it makes the difference.
- Taking breaks, breathing deeply, and staying organized can reduce overwhelming feelings.
- Managing stress now builds resilience for the future.

Mini-FAQ

Q1: How can I stop feeling stressed all the time?
A: Identify what's in your control, break big tasks into smaller ones, and use grounding techniques to reset.

Q2: Isn't stress just part of life?
A: Yes, but you can learn to manage it so it doesn't take over your life.

Managing stress is a powerful skill, but true confidence comes from believing in yourself. In the next chapter, we'll explore how to build lasting confidence.

11

BUILDING SELF-BELIEF

Confidence isn't about waking up every morning feeling like the main character in an action movie. It's not about never doubting yourself or always having the perfect comeback. Confidence is believing in yourself enough to try, even when your brain is whispering, "*What if I fail?*" It's about knowing that even if things don't go perfectly, you'll figure it out, adjust, and keep moving forward.

Think of confidence as your personal WiFi signal, sometimes it's strong, sometimes it's spotty, but the more you strengthen it, the better it works when you need it most. Without confidence, fear of failure or judgment can put you on airplane mode, stopping you from speaking up, taking risks, or chasing after what you really want. And honestly? You deserve better than that.

The Truth About Confidence: It's Built, Not Born

The good news? Confidence isn't a personality trait, it's a skill. And like any skill, it gets stronger the more you practice. Dr. Albert Bandura, a psychologist known for his work on self-efficacy, discovered that the best way to build confidence is through small wins.

Each time you push yourself just a little outside your comfort zone, whether that's raising your hand in class, trying something new, or simply not deleting that text out of overthinking panic, you prove to yourself that you are capable. And every small victory? It adds up to the kind of confidence that makes you unstoppable.

The Science Behind Confidence: Rewiring Your Brain

Your brain is like a muscle, and every time you challenge yourself, it strengthens the neural pathways that make confidence easier the next time around.

Neuroplasticity is the brain's ability to change and adapt based on experiences. The more you practice confidence-building actions, raising your hand in class, speaking up, trying new things, the stronger your confidence "muscle" becomes.

Why does this matter? Because if you've ever thought, I'll never be confident, science disagrees. Your brain is designed to learn and improve, you just have to give it the right training.

The Bigger Picture: How Confidence Prepares You for Life

Mastering confidence now doesn't just help you speak up in class, it's setting the stage for bigger things in your future. Confidence affects everything, from getting opportunities to handling setbacks like a pro.

Here's how confidence gives you a real-world edge:

1. Better Performance in School & Work – Confident people take on challenges instead of avoiding them (which means they learn faster and grow faster).
2. Stronger Social Skills – Confidence helps you connect with others, build relationships, and make great first impressions.
3. Resilience & Growth – When you believe in yourself, failures don't define you, they become learning experiences.
4. Greater Opportunities – People with confidence go for things, leadership roles, internships, creative projects, while self-doubt holds others back.

What Low Confidence Feels Like in the Body

When your confidence levels are running on low battery mode, it doesn't just stay in your head, it shows up everywhere:

- Shaky voice or avoiding eye contact – Like your body is screaming *"I don't belong here!"* when you totally do.
- Racing heart & sweaty palms – Because apparently, your body thinks introducing yourself in a group is the same as being chased by a bear.
- Overthinking & doubting your abilities – Turning *"I made a mistake"* into *"I am a mistake"* (which is not true, by the way!).
- Fear of failure or embarrassment – Feeling like if you mess up even once, everyone will remember it forever (spoiler: they won't).

The Bottom Line? Confidence is a Muscle, Use It or Lose It

Confidence isn't about never feeling nervous or uncertain, it's about trusting yourself enough to act anyway. The more you practice stepping up, speaking out, and betting on yourself, the stronger that confidence muscle gets. So go ahead, take that small risk, raise your hand, post that creative idea, and remind yourself: You are capable. You are worthy. And you've got this.

Expert Advice

Dr. Amy Cuddy, a social psychologist, found that body language influences confidence. Studies show that adopting "power poses" for just two minutes can boost confidence and lower stress.

Building Confidence Step by Step

Confidence isn't built overnight, it's developed through action. Here's how you can strengthen your self-belief:

- Practice self-talk: Replace negative thoughts with positive ones. Instead of saying *I can't do this*, say *I can improve with practice.*
- Prepare in advance: Whether it's a speech, a test, or a social event, being prepared helps you feel more in control.
- Step outside your comfort zone: Try new things, even if they scare you a little. Each small success builds confidence.
- Celebrate progress: Acknowledge every achievement, no matter how small. Confidence grows when you recognize your own growth.
- Use power poses: Sit up straight, stand up tall, and walk with confidence.

Actionable Strategies

An Emotions Ninja follows the **Confidence Code**, which includes three essential steps to building lasting confidence:

1. **Picture Yourself Succeeding** – Visualization is a powerful tool. Before a big challenge, close your eyes and imagine yourself succeeding. See yourself delivering a great speech, scoring the winning goal, or making a new friend. This mental preparation helps your brain feel more comfortable and reduces fear.
2. **Practice Failing** – Confidence isn't about never failing, it's about getting comfortable with failure. The more you expose yourself to challenges, the easier it becomes to handle setbacks. Try something new, embrace mistakes, and learn from them instead of fearing them.
3. **Put Your Goals Down on Paper**– Writing down your goals increases the chances of achieving them. Draw a rocket and list your top three confidence-building goals. For example, "Raise my hand in class once a day," "Try out for a new club," or "Speak up when I have an idea." Seeing your goals on paper makes them feel real and achievable.

Other ways to build confidence include:

- Posture Power: Standing tall with shoulders back can actually trick your brain into feeling more confident.
- Visualization: Picture yourself succeeding before you even try.
- Speaking Up: Practice expressing your opinions, even in small ways.
- Try these confidence-building techniques and see how they transform your self-belief!

Relatable Teen Scenarios for Confidence

Scenario 1: Speaking Up in Class

Your teacher asks a question, and you know the answer, but you hesitate. *What if I get it wrong? What if people think I sound dumb?* Your heart races, and you decide to stay quiet instead.

Reframing the Thought: Instead of assuming the worst, you remind yourself, *Even if I get it wrong, it's okay, learning is part of growing*. The next time your teacher asks a question, you raise your hand. Even though you feel nervous, you speak up, and it boosts your confidence for next time.

Scenario 2: Trying Out for a Team or Club

You want to join the soccer team or audition for the school play, but self-doubt creeps in: I'm probably not good enough. *What if I embarrass myself?* You consider skipping the tryouts just to avoid failure.

Reframing the Thought: Instead of focusing on what could go wrong, you tell yourself, *Even if I don't make it, I'll never know unless I try*. You step outside your comfort zone, give it your best shot, and realize that having the courage to try is already a success, whether you make the team or not.

Scenario 3: Handling Rejection

You apply for a leadership position at school, and you're excited and hopeful. But when the results come out, your name isn't on the list. *Maybe I'm just not good enough*, you think. You start questioning yourself and wondering if you should stop trying for things like this.

Reframing the Thought: Instead of seeing rejection as a failure, you remind yourself, *This one moment doesn't define me. I can learn from this and come back stronger.* You talk to a teacher or mentor for feedback, use it to improve, and keep going.

Scenario 4: Feeling Confident in Your Own Skin

You scroll through social media and see people looking perfect, achieving things, and living amazing lives. You compare yourself and start thinking, *I'll never be that good-looking/smart/talented.* Your confidence drops instantly.

Reframing the Thought: Instead of comparing, you remind yourself, *Social media isn't real life. My strengths, talents, and personality make me unique.* You put the phone down, focus on what you love about yourself, and start celebrating your own progress instead of comparing it to others.

"Confidence comes not from always being right but from not fearing to be wrong." — Peter T. McIntyre

Personal Story

When I was younger, I struggled with confidence, especially when it came to public speaking. I remember one particular moment in school that stuck with me for years.

It was the day of my first big presentation. I had spent hours preparing, practicing my speech in front of the mirror, and writing everything down so I wouldn't forget. But as soon as I stood in front of the class, my mind went blank. My heart pounded, my palms got sweaty, and all I could think was, Everyone is staring at me. What if I mess up?

I stumbled through the first few sentences, but the panic in my head only got louder. I was so nervous that I rushed through the entire speech, barely looking up from my paper. When I finally sat down, I felt embarrassed and disappointed in myself. I thought, Maybe I'm just not good at public speaking. Maybe I never will be.

For a long time, I avoided speaking in front of people. But then, something changed. A teacher noticed my hesitation and gave me some advice that I'll never forget: Confidence isn't about never feeling nervous, it's about pushing through fear anyway. She encouraged me to practice failing on purpose, to try speaking out in small ways, even if I didn't feel ready.

I started raising my hand more in class, even when my voice shook. I volunteered for small speaking roles, even if I doubted myself. Little by little, my confidence grew. The next time I had to give a presentation, I still felt nervous, but this time, I knew I could handle it.

Fast forward to today, I've spoken in front of hundreds of people at events, and I even teach others how to build confidence. But if you had told me back then that I would one day love public speaking, I never would have believed you. I learned that confidence isn't about being fearless, it's about taking action even when fear is there.

Confidence is built, not born, and every small step forward makes you stronger.

Ninja Wisdom

Confidence isn't about being fearless, it's about knowing you can handle whatever comes your way. Confidence isn't about never failing, it's about knowing you can handle whatever comes your way.

Case Study: The Self-Doubt Battle

Tyler doubted his basketball skills and always benched himself, before the coach even could. One day, a teammate told him, "Confidence isn't being the best, it's showing up and trying." Tyler decided to practice instead of sitting out, and guess what? He made a game-winning shot at practice. That moment taught him that confidence isn't about being perfect, it's about taking the shot, even if you miss a few.

Quick Quiz Box

Which of the following helps build confidence?

- a) Practicing something repeatedly
- b) Avoiding challenges to stay comfortable
- c) Focusing only on past failures
- d) Comparing yourself to others

(Answer: a) Practicing something repeatedly)

Journal Reflection Box

Write about a time you felt confident. What helped you feel that way? How can you apply that to other areas of your life?

Action Challenge Chart

Situation	Negative Thought	Confidence-Building Action
Speaking in class	What if I sound dumb?	Take a deep breath and share my thoughts
Trying a new sport	I'll embarrass myself	Remember that everyone starts somewhere
Making new friends	They won't like me	Focus on being friendly and open

Develop confidence with these strategies next time you're feeling unsure.

Chapter 11 Key Takeaways

- Confidence isn't about never doubting yourself, it's about taking action anyway.
- Small successes build confidence over time.
- Your brain rewires itself as you practice confidence (thanks, neuroplasticity!).

Mini-FAQ

Q1: What if I just don't feel confident?
A: Confidence comes from doing, start small, take tiny risks, and watch your confidence grow.

Q2: What if people judge me?
A: People are too busy worrying about themselves. Focus on your own growth rather than outside opinions.

Confidence helps us take action, but what if shyness holds us back? In the next chapter, we'll learn F.U.N. steps to help you speak up and embrace your quiet strength."

12

EMBRACING YOUR QUIET STRENGTH

You know that moment when someone invites you to join a conversation, and your heart does a weird somersault? Or when you want to speak up in class but feel like your words are stuck behind a locked door in your throat? That's shyness stepping in. Here's the truth: being shy isn't automatically bad. In fact, it can be a sign you're thoughtful and observant, the type of person who listens deeply before speaking.

But when extreme shyness keeps you from hanging out with friends, joining activities you love, or even raising your hand in class for fear of looking "silly," that's when it becomes a roadblock. Shy Ninja helps you understand that it's perfectly okay to enjoy your quiet space; you just don't want to miss out on life because your nerves decide to hog the spotlight.

Different Shades of Shyness

Not all shyness looks the same. You might see yourself in one or more of these:

1. The Wallflower Watcher
   » You're happiest on the sidelines, observing the scene. You can be incredibly insightful, but at times, that caution keeps you from diving in and experiencing the fun firsthand.
2. The Awkward Ice-Breaker Avoider
   » Starting a conversation feels like scaling Mount Everest. It's not that you hate people; you just freeze when it comes to saying hello or introducing yourself.
3. The Stage-Fright Survivor
   » You're fine chatting with friends but clam up if you have to speak or perform in front of an audience, whether that's giving a presentation or reading a poem.
4. The One-on-One Expert
   » You shine in small, intimate groups but feel overwhelmed in bigger settings, like parties, clubs, or bustling classrooms.

Being shy can mean you're a deep thinker, a great listener, or someone who prefers a smaller social circle, and that's awesome. The challenge is making sure your shyness doesn't turn into a cage that stops you from exploring new opportunities.

The Sneaky Consequences of Extreme Shyness

When shyness takes the wheel, it can quietly steer you away from experiences that could help you grow and connect:

- Missed Opportunities: You might avoid volunteering for leadership roles, missing a chance to develop cool skills.
- Stifled Self-Expression: Holding your thoughts inside means people miss out on your insights, humor, or creativity. Your unique perspective never sees the light of day.
- Communication Anxiety: Fear of public speaking or even small talk can turn daily activities, like ordering food or participating in a classroom discussion, into mini panic events.

- Low Self-Confidence: Constantly avoiding interactions can make you feel like you're incapable or invisible, setting off a cycle where you doubt yourself more and more.
- Isolation: Over time, extreme shyness can lead to feeling lonely or cut off from social circles, even if you crave companionship deep down.

It's one thing to enjoy solitude or prefer smaller groups; it's another to hide from the world because shyness is telling you you're not worthy or you'll say something dumb. That's where things get sneaky, and that's exactly what Shy Ninja wants to help you overcome.

What Extreme Shyness Feels Like in the Body

If you've ever faced a social interaction that made you want to vanish, you know the physical punch shyness can pack:

- Tense Shoulders & Neck: Your muscles clench up, bracing for an imaginary danger.
- Blushing & Sweaty Palms: The classic signs of your sympathetic nervous system going into overdrive, announcing "Alert! Alert!" even if there's no real threat.
- Racing Heartbeat: Your heart works overtime, as though running a marathon without leaving your chair.
- Queasy Stomach: That dreaded swirl of nerves can make food the last thing on your mind.
- Shallow Breathing: You catch yourself taking quick, small breaths, which ironically can make you feel even more light-headed and anxious.

These sensations aren't here to torture you, they're your body's way of saying, "This situation feels unfamiliar or risky." Once you realize what's happening, you can begin to gently push past the fear and step into moments of confidence.

Ready to see how a Shy Ninja turns nervous butterflies into gentle nudges toward social growth? Next up, we'll explore expert advice and actionable strategies to help you find balance, where you can still cherish your quiet strengths and join in on the everyday magic of connecting with people. Because life is way too big and bright to watch from the sidelines forever.

Expert Advice

Behavioral psychologists suggest that gradually exposing yourself to social situations you find intimidating is one of the best ways to reduce shyness. Small steps, like chatting with one new person or raising your hand once in class, can desensitize you to the anxiety that used to hold you back.

Actionable Strategies

An Emotions Ninja remembers that things can be **F.U.N.**

1. **F – Focus**
   - First, focus on your breathing.
   - Slow, controlled breaths calm the racing thoughts and jitters, giving you a moment to gather yourself before stepping into a conversation or activity.
2. **U – Use**
   - Next, use positive mantras.
   - Simple, encouraging statements remind you that you're capable of handling the moment. Even if your voice shakes a bit at first, repeating "I can try!" helps you push through the hesitation.
3. **N – Nudge**
   - And finally, nudge your fears aside.
   - Challenge your anxious what-ifs by easing into the situation. Say hello, offer a smile, or ask a question. Each nudge forward weakens the hold shyness has on you.

Armed with the F.U.N. method, let's explore how these steps can support you in everyday moments when shyness tries to hold you back.

Relatable Teen Scenarios for Shyness

Scenario 1: New Club, New Faces

You walk into the art club for the first time, feeling like everyone already knows each other.

Making the Wise Choice: By focusing on your breathing (F), repeating "I can try!" (U), and nudging yourself to ask how someone learned their cool painting technique (N), you crack open the door to new friendships.

Scenario 2: Group Presentation Nerves

Your teacher assigns group presentations, and you dread speaking up.

Making the Wise Choice: Take a few breaths before presenting (F), remind yourself "I'm prepared for this!" (U), then nudge yourself to deliver that first sentence with conviction (N).

"You wouldn't worry so much about what others think of you if you realized how seldom they do."
- Eleanor Roosevelt

Personal Story: Shy Me

I still remember the day I tried to blurt out a joke in a big group of friends, only to have my mind blank out mid-sentence. I stood there, mouth half-open, feeling my cheeks heat up like overripe tomatoes, while everyone stared at me in confusion. One friend actually leaned forward as though encouraging my words to keep going, but they'd abandoned ship entirely. I mumbled something about "never mind," let out the most awkward laugh known to humanity, and practically sprinted away.

At home, I replayed the scene roughly 200 times, just in case I could find a new angle to be mortified from. I felt like a social disaster, convinced everyone thought I was the weirdo who couldn't finish a sentence. But here's the twist: a few days later, one of the same friends who witnessed that fiasco casually texted me, "Hey, that half-joke you tried to say the other day? I bet it was hilarious, care to share it now?"

Turns out, no one was judging me as harshly as I'd been judging myself. I typed my little joke out (it was something silly about how the cafeteria pizza tasted like actual cardboard, but I had a zinger about dipping sauce) and sent it. She replied with a series of laughing emojis, like, actual hysterical-laughter emojis. Suddenly, that mortifying moment felt more like a bonding mishap than an eternal stamp of "shy-person failure."

Looking back, I learned two big things: first, my shyness was totally normal, everyone blanks sometimes, especially in bigger groups. Second, even if you stumble over your words, the people who really matter will lean in, not back. Sometimes a half-formed joke can turn into a full friendship, as long as you're willing to share your voice, even when it feels like your nerves are doing the tango in your stomach. It's okay to be shy, to have an awkward moment or two (or ten), and to laugh about it afterward. If anything, a red face and a forgotten punchline can spark empathy, and a new inside joke, faster than any perfectly polished line ever could.

If I'd used F.U.N. that day, maybe I would've finished the

joke, and discovered my friend group loves a good laugh as much as I do!

Ninja Wisdom

Courage isn't the absence of fear, it's moving forward while you're afraid.

Case Study: The Classroom Q&A

Ali always knew the answers in class but never raised her hand. She practiced F.U.N.: focusing on three calming breaths, telling herself, "I've got this," and nudging her hand in the air. The first time was nerve-wracking, but after a few tries, she realized she could handle the spotlight. Her participation soared, and so did her grades.

Quick Quiz Box

Which of the following is part of the F.U.N. method?
• a) Flee the scene as quickly as possible
• b) Use negative self-talk to prepare
• c) Focus on your breathing, use mantras, and nudge yourself to act
• d) Never speak unless spoken to

(Answer: c. Focusing, using positive mantras, and nudging forward are the key steps.)

Journal Reflection Box

Think of a situation where your shyness held you back. How can you apply F.U.N. to handle it differently next time?

Action Challenge Chart

Shy Moment	F.U.N. Step in Action	Outcome / Feeling
Sitting alone at lunch	Focus (3 deep breaths), then whisper "I can try!" to yourself; nudge by asking to join a table	Met new people, felt proud
Avoiding a school dance	Use the mantra "I deserve to have fun" (U), then nudge by attending for at least 30 minutes	Discovered dancing isn't so scary
Hesitant to ask teacher a question	Breathe calmly (F), say "I can learn this!" (U), walk up to the teacher's desk (N)	Got the help you needed, gained confidence

An Emotions Ninja embraces the F.U.N. method, because with a little focus, a supportive mantra, and that gentle nudge forward, you can make friends, speak your mind, and find joy in social settings you once dreaded. You're just one breath and one mantra away from stepping out of your shell!

Chapter 12 Key Takeaways

- Shyness Isn't a Flaw. It can reflect depth and thoughtfulness.
- F.U.N.. Focus on breathing, Use mantras, Nudge yourself to act.
- Small Steps Count. Quietly trying one new social action builds confidence over time.

Mini-FAQ

Q1: I'm too anxious to even try a 'small step.' Any advice?
A: Start smaller. Practice a greeting in the mirror or with someone you trust. Even a single, gentle wave at school is progress. F.U.N. is all about micro-moves.

Q2: Won't people think I'm weird if I suddenly start talking more?
A: Most people welcome friendly engagement. A shift from silence to speaking up can be surprising at first, but genuine curiosity or kindness usually draws positive responses.

You've completed your journey through mastering emotions! In the final section, we'll reflect on everything you've learned and how to continue growing as an Emotions Ninja.

FINAL THOUGHTS

YOUR JOURNEY TO EMOTIONAL STRENGTH

A Note from Me to You

Life isn't always easy. Some days, your emotions lift you up, pushing you to dream big and connect deeply. Other days, they feel like an unstoppable storm, pulling you in different directions. But here's what I want you to remember: You are not your emotions. You feel them, but they don't define you. You are in control. You are an expert Emotions Ninja now.

Every challenge, every emotion, every experience has shaped you into the incredible person you are meant to be. And guess what? You're still growing.

This book isn't meant to be read once and put away. Keep it close, on your desk, by your bedside, in your backpack, so that when life feels overwhelming, you have a reminder of your strength. Your emotions don't control you, you have the tools to take charge, face obstacles, and navigate life with confidence.

Throughout these chapters, you've gained the tools to:

- Manage frustration and anger without losing control
- Turn stress into motivation instead of overwhelming feelings

- Build confidence, even when self-doubt creeps in
- Embrace patience, kindness, and resilience in everyday life
- Recognize that your emotions are signals, not threats

You now know that emotions aren't something to fear, they're a guide, helping you understand yourself and the world around you.

Your Next Steps

1. Practice daily. Emotional growth isn't a one-time thing. The more you use these strategies, the stronger your emotional intelligence will become.
2. Give yourself grace. You won't always get it right, and that's okay. Mistakes = growth.
3. Seek support. You don't have to do life alone. Lean on friends, family, teachers, or mentors when you need guidance.
4. Reflect often. Take time to recognize how far you've come. Growth happens little by little, day by day.

You've Got This!

You are not your emotions. You have the power to change your thoughts, shift your perspective, and build the life you want, one choice at a time. This book was just the beginning. Now, it's time to take what you've learned and make it your own. The world needs your unique light. So go out there and shine.

With encouragement and support,
Mary Nhin

FINAL REFLECTIONS

YOUR EMOTIONAL GROWTH JOURNEY

Biggest Takeaway Reflection

Take a moment to reflect on everything you've learned in this book. What stood out the most to you? Maybe it was a strategy that helped you manage stress, a perspective shift that made you rethink your emotions, or an actionable tip that made your day easier.

Write down your biggest takeaway from this book:

_____

_____

Personal Growth Plan: Setting Your Emotional Intelligence Goals

Emotional intelligence isn't something you learn once, it's something you build over time. Now that you have new tools and strategies, let's set 2-3 personal growth goals to continue your journey.

Goal #1: One emotional habit I want to improve:

_____

Goal #2: One strategy I will practice regularly:

_____

Goal #3: One way I will be kinder to myself when I struggle:

_____

Remember: Growth happens in small, daily steps. Keep this page somewhere visible and check in with yourself regularly. You have everything you need to continue strengthening your emotional intelligence and living with confidence, resilience, and self-awareness. Your journey doesn't end here, it's just beginning!

NINJA MOVES GLOSSARY

Kind Ninja – G.I.F.T.

G – Give Without Expecting: Kindness is most powerful when given freely, not for attention or reward.
I – Include Others: Small gestures, like inviting someone to sit with you, can make people feel valued.
F – Find Opportunities: Look for ways to help, whether it's holding the door or offering a smile.
T – Take Time to Appreciate: Acknowledge acts of kindness from others and return the favor.

Angry Ninja – 1 + 3 + 10 Rule

1 – Say one calming word like "Relax" or "Breathe."
3 – Take three deep breaths to slow down your emotions.
10 – Count to ten before responding to give yourself space to think before acting.

CBT Ninja – Thoughts, Feelings, Behaviors

Thoughts: Recognize negative thoughts when they appear. Challenge them by asking, Is this true?

Feelings: Observe how your thoughts affect your emotions. A single thought can make you feel anxious, confident, or discouraged.
Behaviors: Change your response by shifting your mindset. When you think positively, you feel better and make better choices.

Anxious Ninja – The 3 Rs

R – Recognize: Identify when anxiety is starting to build up.
R – Relax: Use grounding techniques, deep breathing, or stretching to calm your body.
R – Refocus: Shift your attention to what you can control instead of worrying about what you can't.

Happy Ninja – D.O.S.E.

D – Dopamine: Boost motivation by setting small goals and celebrating wins.
O – Oxytocin: Strengthen relationships by connecting with loved ones and practicing kindness.
S – Serotonin: Improve mood through gratitude, positive thinking, and spending time in nature.
E – Endorphins: Lift your energy and reduce stress by laughing, exercising, or doing something fun.

Sad Ninja – S.A.D.

S – Share Your Feelings: Talk to someone you trust about what's making you sad.
A – Allow Yourself to Feel: It's okay to cry or take time to process emotions.
D – Do Something That Brings Comfort: Listen to music, go for a walk, or engage in a hobby you love.

Patient Ninja – The 3 Ts

T – Think Through the Consequences: Before making a rash decision, consider the long-term impact.

T – Tell Yourself to Wait: Remind yourself that patience leads to better outcomes.
T – Take Deep Breaths: Use breathing techniques to stay calm and avoid impulsive reactions.

Worry Ninja – The Circle of Control and Dandelion

The Circle of Control: Write down worries and separate them into things you can control vs. things you can't. Focus your energy where it matters.

Dandelion Technique: Visualize your worries as dandelion seeds. Take a deep breath, and as you exhale, imagine those worries floating away with the wind.

Positive Ninja – Deep Breath Reset:

When negativity creeps in, inhale deeply for four seconds, hold for seven, and exhale for eight. This signals your brain to reset and refocus.

Stressed Ninja – Grounding

Engage your senses to bring yourself back to the present.
Five things you see
Four things you touch
Three things you hear
Two things you smell
One thing you taste

Confident Ninja – Confidence Code

Picture Yourself Succeeding: Visualize yourself handling challenges with confidence.

Practice Failing: Confidence grows when you get comfortable with mistakes and learn from them.

Put Your Goals on Paper: Writing down your goals makes them more tangible and achievable. Seeing your progress builds belief in yourself

Shy Ninja – F.U.N.

F - Focus: Use slow, controlled breathing to calm your nerves.
U - Use: Positive self-talk ("I can try!") when anxiety creeps in.
N - Nudge: Take small steps out of your comfort zone, say hello, ask a question, smile first.

    You've learned so much, now take these Ninja Moves into the real world!

HELP AND SUPPORT RESOURCES

If you or someone you know is feeling lost, overwhelmed, or unsure of what to do, know that help is available. Many organizations and individuals are ready to support you.

Please reach out by calling or visiting the resources listed below. If the first attempt doesn't provide the help you need, don't lose hope, keep trying. You are not alone.

For any life-threatening crisis call

CRISIS CALL CENTER (available 24/7)
📞 1-800-273-8255 or text ANSWER to 839863

Substance Abuse

If you or a friend may be struggling with drug or alcohol use and are unsure what to do, reach out by calling or visiting:
National Council on Alcoholism and Drug Abuse
📞 1-800-622-2255
➡ www.ncadd.org

If you're concerned about a family member or friend struggling with alcohol or drug use and don't know how to help, reach out by calling or visiting:

Al-Anon/Alateen
📞 1-888-425-2666
➡ www.al-anon.alateen.org

For information about drugs, alcohol, and tobacco, reach out by calling or visiting:

The American Council for Drug Education
📞 1-888-286-5027
➡ www.phoenixhouse.org

Partnership for a Drug-Free America
📞 1-855-DRUGFREE
➡ www.drugfree.org

Eating Disorders

If you or a friend may be experiencing anorexia, bulimia, or an overeating disorder and need support, reach out by calling or visiting:

National Eating Disorders Association
📞 1-800-931-2237
➡ www.nationaleatingdisorders.org

Physical and Mental Health

If you or a friend are considering suicide, PLEASE call the Crisis Call Center or visit:

Suicide Hotline
📞 1-800-273-TALK
➡ www.afsp.org

For more information about depression or mental illnesses, creach out by calling or visiting:

National Institute of Mental Health Information Center
📞 1-866-615-6464
➡ www.nimh.nih.gov

If you or your friends are concerned about contracting or having an STD or AIDS, reach out by calling or visiting:

Sexually Transmitted Diseases
📞 1-800-227-8929
➡ www.cdc.gov/STD

National AIDS Hotline
📞 1-800-232-4636
➡ www.cdcnpin.org/hiv/

Grief and Loss

If you or a friend are struggling with a tragedy or the loss of a loved one and don't know how to cope, reach out by calling or visiting:

Tragedy Assistance Program for Survivors
📞 1-800-959-8277
➡ www.taps.org

Teen Pregnancy

If you are pregnant or worried about becoming pregnant and need more information about your options, reach out by calling or visiting:

American Pregnancy Helpline
📞 1-866-942-6466
➡ www.thehelpline.org

Birthright International
📞 1-800-550-4900
➡ www.birthright.org

If you have a baby now or are having a baby, reach out by calling or visiting:

Baby Your Baby
📞 1-800-826-9662
➡ www.babyyourbaby.org

Abuse

If you are in a dating relationship with an abusive person, reach out by calling or visiting:

National Teen Dating Abuse Helpline
📞 1-866-331-9474
➡ www.loveisrespect.org

If you or a friend, male or female, are a victim of rape, incest, or any form of sexual abuse, reach out by calling or visiting:

Rape, Abuse, and Incest National Network
📞 1-800-656-4673
➡ www.rainn.org

If you or a friend or any family member is being abused at home, reach out by calling or visiting:

National Domestic Violence Hotline
📞 1-800-799-7233
➡ www.ndvh.org

If you or a friend is being bullied, creach out by calling or visiting:

Speak Up: School Violence and Bullying
📞 1-866-773-2587
➡ www.cpyv.org

If you or a friend is being cyberbullied, visit:
www.stopbullying.gov/cyberbullying/

Or call: Cyber Tipline
📞 1-800-843-5678
➡ www.cybertipline.com

Gang Prevention

Boys and Girls Club of America
Find a club near you:
➡ www.bgca.org

Education

If you're worried about how to pay for college or future career training, reach out by calling or visiting:

Educational Funding
📞 1-800-USA-LEARN / 1-800-725-3276
➡ www.ed.gov

Federal Student Aid
📞 1-800-4-FED AID / 1-800-433-3243
➡ www.fafsa.ed.gov

If you want to learn how to handle money wisely or save for your future, visit:
➡ www.mymoney.gov

Volunteerism

If you and your friends are interested in making a difference and learning leadership skills at the same time, reach out by calling or visiting:

YMCA
📞 1-800-872-9622
➡ www.ymca.net

America's Charities
📞 1-800-458-9505
➡ www.charities.org

United Way
Find United Way in your community:
➡ www.unitedway.org

General Youth Support Services

If you're a runaway and need help or want to return home, reach out by calling or visiting:

National Runaway Safeline
📞 1-800-RUNAWAY
➡ www.1800runaway.org

If you're homeless and need somewhere to stay, food to eat, and crisis care, reach out by calling or visiting:

Covenant House Nine-Line
📞 1-800-999-9999
➡ www.covenanthouse.org

If you think you may have a problem with online gaming addiction, reach out by calling or visiting:

On-Line Gamers Anonymous
➡ www.olganon.org

If you need help working something out or just need to talk to someone, reach out by calling or visiting:

Teen Line
📞 1-800-TLC-TEEN
➡ https://teenlineonline.org/talk-now
Or text 'teen' to 839863

BOOKS & RESOURCES MENTIONED IN THIS BOOK

If you're interested in diving deeper into emotions, mindset, and self-improvement, check out these insightful books and research-backed resources from leading psychologists and experts:

Feeling Good: The New Mood Therapy – Dr. David Burns
A groundbreaking book on cognitive behavioral therapy (CBT) that teaches how to challenge and reframe negative thoughts to improve mood and mental well-being.

The Science of Kindness – Dr. David Hamilton
Explores how small acts of kindness can improve physical and mental health, strengthen the immune system, and reduce anxiety and depression.

Under Pressure: Confronting the Epidemic of Stress and Anxiety in Girls – Dr. Lisa Damour
A must-read on how anxiety can be a sign of growth and how teens can develop resilience by facing their fears instead of avoiding them.

The Happiness Lab (Podcast & Course) – Dr. Laurie Santos
Based on Yale's most popular course, this resource explores the science of happiness and how daily habits like gratitude and mindfulness can improve well-being.

The Marshmallow Test: Mastering Self-Control – Dr. Walter Mischel
Reveals the science behind self-discipline and how delaying gratification leads to greater success in school, relationships, and life.

Unwinding Anxiety – Dr. Judson Brewer
A neuroscientist's guide to understanding anxiety as a habit loop and how curiosity can help break the cycle of worry.

Presence: Bringing Your Boldest Self to Your Biggest Challenges – Dr. Amy Cuddy
Explains how body language and power poses can boost confidence and lower stress, making it easier to handle difficult emotions.

Anger Control: The Power of Self-Talk – Dr. Raymond Novaco
A deep dive into anger management, offering self-talk strategies to stay in control when emotions run high.

Each of these books and resources provides science-backed strategies to help navigate emotions, build confidence, and develop a resilient mindset. Which one will you explore first?

A Special Thank You to My Team of Ninjas

Forrest Weston | Emily Keller | Sarah Altman | Jen B | Deborah Lennon | Melissa Thompson | Jennifer Coots | Desiree Trott | Bridget Jackson | Nancy Grim | Tomasine Oliphant, MSW | Trinity Winkers | Stacey Scott | Brandy L. Taylor | Joaquin Gabriel | Melinda Hubble | Christina Lauricella | Lindsey Birrel, SSW | Kaitlyn Hope Partin | Elana Reynolds | Beau Tra | Susan M. Hall | Samantha Spiegel | Anna Pack | The Prince Family | Anna Lee Velasco | Connie Young | Becky Turner | Benedicte | Britany Doan | Luke Newcomb | Anne Marie Bishop | Sarah Kilroy | Danielle G | Aiko | Nicole Campbell | Layla Touchet | Eli | Chris Bulinksi | Heather Speer, MSW, LICSW | Teresa Dehning | Sarah Bie | Bethany Lockhart, LCSW | Kathy Connelly | Mason Nguyen | Racheal Malet | Jackie Minkalis | T. Coulombe | Scott Strine, Director Effingham Community Library | Dee La | Asa River King | Ally Braun | Tara Baker | Brandy Hughes | Melissa Bedford, LPC | Devony Arrington | Rebecca, Lachlan, and Meredith Nirschl | Sarah Fred | Kimberly Hughes | Devony Arrington | Katherine Y | Natalie Marquis

Other Products by Mary Nhin

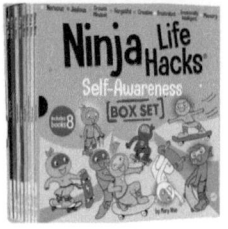 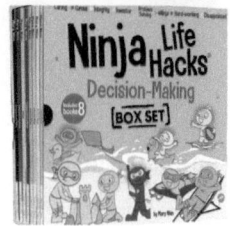 
 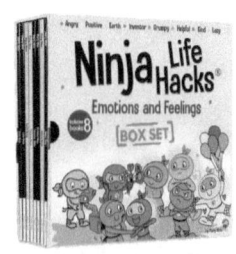 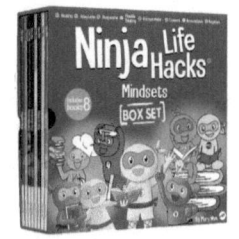

NinjaLifeHacks.tv

About the Author

Mary Nhin is a social impact entrepreneur and author of the flagship series, Ninja Life Hacks, a social-emotional learning brand, with 124 books and 99 characters, dedicated to empowering children with life skills. It's captured the hearts of over four million readers and continues to lead the way for an exciting adventure in social, emotional learning.

At the core of Mary Nhin's writing is a flicker of hope. While the writer frequently lays her soul bare, tackling issues such as failures, acceptance, and loneliness, there's always a silver lining. That's particularly true of her book series, "Ninja Life Hacks," which looks at failures as a transformative experience.

Under Mary's leadership, the Ninja Life Hacks brand of books, resources, and toys have empowered people worldwide with social, emotional coping strategies to use for a lifetime. Her books have been translated in twelve countries.

As Co-founder and Chief Creative Officer of Nhinja Sushi, the mom and pop restaurant has blossomed into a five location restaurant chain, serving up high quality sushi and freshly cooked meals to busy families. Today, over 1500+ people visit Nhinja locations daily.

Mary's visionary leadership earned her and her teams a collection of industry accolades including: Woman of Integrity Award Winner (Better Business Bureau), Most Admired CEO (The Journal Record), HER award (405 Magazine), Top 50 Most Influential Oklahomans Power List (Journal Record), Top 100

Small Businesses (U.S. Chamber of Commerce), AAPI Strong Restaurant Winner (National ACE), In the Lead Female Leader (Journal Record), 40 Under Forty (OKC Business), Inc 5000 (Inc. Magazine), Best Sushi (Edmond Life and Leisure and Edmond Sun), Best Finance Books For Kids (Investopedia), Best Kids Money Books (Mom.com).

She and her husband, Kang Nhin, are proud parents of three children, Mikey, Kobe, and Jojo.

WEBSITE: www.ninjalifehacks.tv

WEBSITE: www.nhinja.com

LINKEDIN: @Marynhin

FB: Nhinja Sushi

FB: Ninja Life Hacks

IG: @nhinjasushi

IG: @officialninjalifehacks

TT: @officialninjalifehacks

YT: youtube.com/@NinjaLifeHacks

X: @nhinjas

Email: mary@ninjalifehacks.tv

www.ingramcontent.com/pod-product-compliance
Lightning Source LLC
LaVergne TN
LVHW041945070526
838199LV00051BA/2909